HULL TO HORNSEA & WITHERNSEA

plus the Spurn Head Railway

Vic Mitchell and Keith Smith

MP Middleton Press

Front cover: Hornsea is seen not long before closure, with a DMU bearing the much-admired 'Cats Whiskers'. Gas lamps prevail and snakes support the seat. (Colour-Rail.com)

Back cover (upper): Examples of the use of sail power are shown in the final pages of this album and so here is the only working example in the UK now. Vic Mitchell is by Spooner's Boat in 2017 at Minffordd, on the Festiniog Railway. It can be viewed at the Victorian Weekend each October. For details telephone 01766 516024 or visit: www.festrail.co.uk. *(S.Morgan)*

Back cover (lower): The Railway Clearing House map of 1947 has the North Sea on the right and the River Hull meandering from the north.

Published March 2019
First reprint April 2020
Second reprint November 2020

ISBN 978 1 910356 27 2

© *Middleton Press Ltd, 2019*

Cover design Deborah Esher
Design Cassandra Morgan

Published by
    Middleton Press
    Easebourne Lane
    Midhurst
    West Sussex
    GU29 9AZ
Tel: 01730 813169
Email: info@middletonpress.co.uk
www.middletonpress.co.uk

Printed and bound by CPI Group (UK) Ltd, Croydon, CR0 4YY

CONTENTS

INDEX

ACKNOWLEDGEMENTS

We are very grateful for the assistance received from many of those mentioned in the credits, also from A.J.Castledine, G.Croughton, G.Gartside, A.C.Hartless, J.Hinson (Signalling Record Society), C.M.Howard, N.Langridge, B.Lewis, P. Mathison, M. Nicholson, D. and Dr S. Salter, T.Walsh and, in particular, our always supportive families.

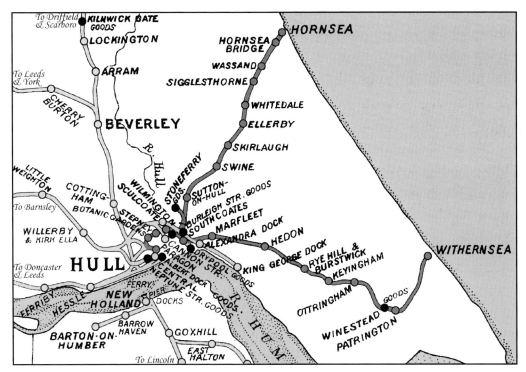

I.   The branches shown on the right of this 1947 Railway Clearing House diagram are those featured herein. The Spurn Head Railway is not shown, as it was not for public use.

GEOGRAPHICAL SETTING

Hull developed near the confluence of the River Humber, from the west, and the River Hull, from the north. A deep-sea fishing port grew and it became a whaling centre also. The location received the name of King's Town, which became Kingston widely. To minimise confusion '-upon-Hull' was added, officially. It received city status in 1897. The abbreviation to just 'Hull' was (and is) common parlance, particularly in the transport world. The lines were built in the county of Yorkshire.

The wide mouth of the Humber was ideal for commercial shipping traffic and docks grew in profusion on the north shore, its geographical position being good in all respects. Holderness forms a long peninsula from the north bank, southwards, terminating at Spurn Head.

The long ferry journey from the south bank was eliminated by the completion of a massive suspension bridge for road traffic in June 1981.

The geology of the area covered by the branches herein is almost entirely boulder clay, the maps showing no contours greater than 50ft above mean sea level.

The Spurn spit of sand and gravel is about 3 miles long, the result of a drift from the coast to the north of it. The peninsula protects the Humber Estuary and is subject to periodic erosion and regrowth, with extensive deposits of sand or clay.

The maps are to the scale of 25ins to 1 mile, with north at the top, unless otherwise indicated.

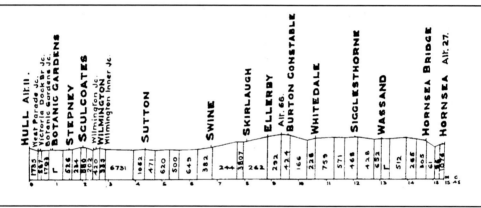

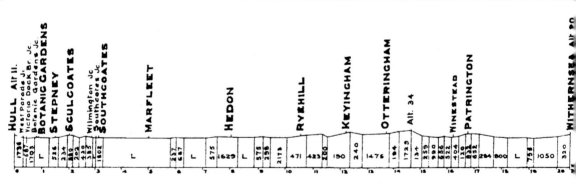

For ferry facilities and connections on the south side of the Humber, see our *Branch Lines North of Grimsby* **album.**

HISTORICAL BACKGROUND

The Hull & Selby Railway arrived from the west through Brough in 1840 and from the north, via Beverley, in 1846. The York & North Midland Railway opened the line into Hull Paragon in 1848. These lines became part of the North Eastern Railway in 1872 and this gained the prefix 'London &' in 1923.

The Hull & Holderness Railway opened its route from Hull to Withernsea on 27th June 1854. However, its trains started from Victoria Dock in Hull until 1st July 1864. The H&HR began services on its branch to Hornsea on 28th March 1864, under an Act of June 1862. It was worked by the NER from the outset, but trains from Hornsea terminated at Wilmington until 1st July 1864. An Act of July 1866 conveyed the line to the NER.

The LNER formed part of the North Eastern Region of British Railways upon nationalisation in 1948 and this included the lines herein. Closure to passengers of both branches took place on 19th October 1964. The area became part of the Eastern Region in 1967. Goods service withdrawals are noted in the captions; all had ceased by 1970, except within Hull itself.

Spurn Head Railway
Howard M. Frost

The Spurn Head Railway was also known as the Spurn Head Military Railway and the Spurn & Kilnsea Railway, the latter name being found on ordnance survey maps of the time. In 1914 it was decided that Hull and the Humber needed a strong defence system. Two large military forts were planned: Spurn Fort for the bulbous tip of the peninsula and Godwin Fort, at Kilnsea.

At that time, there was no road along the peninsula, even though there was a resident population at Spurn Point comprising a full-time lifeboat crew and their families, coastguards, lighthouse keepers, an inn, a post office and a small school. Goods came by boat or had to be carted or carried along the beach. The Hull to Kilnsea road was little more than a track. Most local transport was by horse and cart.

C.J. Wills was appointed as the construction company and it was decided to start with a railway pier at the Point and bring in all the construction materials by boat. The railway was then extended through the sand dunes to Kilnsea. The project was not finished until 1918 or later, but the guns were operational by 1916.

At its height, 2000-3000 service personnel were stationed there. The Army took over a simplified railway system as shown on map XXXIII. However, between the wars the staffing level was reduced to 30-40 Royal Engineers doing maintenance work and during this period a collection of unusual vehicles worked on the line, including sail trolleys. The military occupation was increased for World War II and a concrete road was built during 1940-41. The railway then became less important and was removed in 1951-52. A Bird Observatory was established in 1945 and the Yorkshire Wildlife Trust bought the whole peninsula in 1960. It is now a National Nature Reserve with a visitor centre at the Kilnsea end.

PASSENGER SERVICES

The list below gives a summary of the main services on both routes. Those running on at least five days per week are shown. Details can be found on the tables that follow.

	To Hornsea		To Withernsea	
	Weekdays	Sundays	Weekdays	Sundays
1864	5	1	5	1
1884	7	1	7	1
1904	12	3	13	3
1924	10	3	10	3
1944	7	2	9	2
1961	9	4	11	5

On Summer Saturdays, there were up to 14 extra trains at peak times, serving Withernsea.

HULL and HORNSEA.—North Eastern.

Miles	Down. Paragon Station,	Week Days. mrn	mrn	mrn (Commences on 9th inst.)	mrn	aft	aft (Thurs. & Sats.)	aft	aft	aft	aft	aft (Except Saturdays.)	aft (Except Saturdays.)	aft	aft	aft	aft	aft	Sundays. mrn	aft	aft
	Hull ....dep.	555	8 3	....	9 48	1210	1 35	1e55	2 8	3g30	415	5 0	5 18	550	612	716	9 0	1047	7 50	2 20	7 40
1	Botanic Gardens	559	8 7	9 37	9 52	1214	1 39	1e59	212	3g34	419	....		...	616	...	9 4	1051	7 54	2 24	7 44
1¾	Stepney	6 2	810	9 40	9 55	1217	1 42	2 e 2	215	3g37	422	....		...	619	...	9 7	1054	7 57	2 27	7 47
2¼	Sculcoates	6 5	813	9 42	9 58	1220	....	....	218	3g40	425	....		...	622	...	9 10	....	8 0	2 30	7 50
2½	Wilmington	6 8	816	9 44	10 1	1223	1 46	2 e 6	221	3g43	428	5 6		556	625	722	9 13	1058	8 3	2 33	7 53
4½	Sutton-on-Hull......	613	821		10 6	1228	1 51	....	226	3g48	433	5 11		6 1	630	727	9 18	11 3	8 8	2 38	7 58
7	Swine	619	...		1012	1234		....	232	3g54	439			...	636	...	9 24	11 9	8 14	2 44	8 4
8¼	Skirlaugh	623	...		1016	1238		....	236	3g58	443			...	640	734	9 28	1113	8 18	2 48	8 8
9¾	Burton Constable....	627	830		1020	1242		....	240	4 g 2	447			...	644	738	9 32	1117	8 22	2 52	8 12
10¾	Whitedale	630	833		1023	1245		....	243	4 g 5	450			...	647	...	9 35	1120	8 25	2 55	8 15
12¼	Sigglesthorne	634	837		1027	1249		....	247	4 g 9	454			...	651	...	9 39	....	8 29	2 58	8 18
13	Goxhill	...	...		....	....		....	....	a	...			...	...	...	....	....	....	....	....
15	Hornsea Bridge	640	843	10 3	1033	1255	2 5	2e25	253	4g16	5 0		c	616	657	746	9 45	....	8 35	....	....
15½	Hornsea ....arr.	645	848	10 9	1039	1 0	2 10	2e31	258	4g20	5 5		5 42	620	7 1	750	9 51	1130	8 41	3 11	8 30

Mls	Up.	Week Days. mrn	mrn	mrn	mrn	mrn	mrn	aft	aft	aft	aft	aft	aft	aft	aft	Sundays. mrn	aft	aft	aft
—	Hornsea.........dep.	6 55	7 52	8 30	8 53	9 0	10 50	1 10	3 10	5 15	6 30	7 10	8 e 5	8 15	10 3	9 0	5 20	8 30	8 40
½	Hornsea Bridge	6 58	7 55	8 33	8b56	9 3	10 53	1 13	3 13	5 18	6 33	7 13	8 e 8	8 18	10 6	9 3	....	....	....
2½	Goxhill	....	d	....	....	....	....	....	....	....	....	....	....	....	....	....	....	....	....
3¼	Sigglesthorne	7 5	8 2	....	....	9 9	10 59	1 19	3 19	....	6 39	7 19	....	8 24	10 12	9 9	5 28	....	8 48
4¾	Whitedale	7 9	8 6	8 40	....	....	11 3	1 23	3 23	5 26	....	7 23	....	8 28	10 16	9 13	5 32	....	8 52
5¾	Burton Constable....	7 13	8 10	....	....	9 14	11 6	1 26	3 26	5 29	6 45	7 26	....	8 31	10 19	9 16	5 35	8 40	8 55
7¼	Skirlaugh............	7 18	8 14	....	....	9 18	11 10	1 30	3 30	5 33	....	7 30	....	8 35	10 23	9 20	5 39	....	8 59
8½	Swine................	7 23	8 18	....	....	....	11 14	1 34	3 34	5 37	....	7 34	....	8 39	10 27	9 24	5 43	....	9 3
11	Sutton-on-Hull.......	7 30	8 24	8 49	....	9 25	11 20	1 40	3 40	5 43	6 54	7 40	....	8 45	10 33	9 30	5 49	8 50	9 9
13	Wilmington	7 35	8 29	8 54	....	9 29	11 25	1 45	3 45	5 48	6 59	7 45	8e28	8 50	10 38	9 35	5 54	8 55	9 14
13¾	Sculcoates	7 37	8 31	8 56	....	....	11 27	1 47	3 47	....	7 1	....	....	8 52	....	9 37	5 56	8 57	9 16
14	Stepney (*below*)......	7 40	8 34	....	....	....	11 30	1 50	3 50	5 51	7 4	7 49	8e32	8 55	10 41	9 40	5 59	9 0	9 19
14½	Botanic Gardens	7 42	8 36	8 59	....	....	11 32	1 52	3 52	5 53	7 6	7 51	8e34	8 57	10 43	9 42	6 1	9 2	9 21
15½	**Hull574,569,570**arr.	7 48	8 43	9 6	9 18	9 38	11 38	1 59	3 58	6 0	7 13	7 58	8e41	9 4	10 49	9 48	6 8	9 9	9 28

a Stops to set down from Hull. *b* Stops to take up only. **c** Stops when required to set down.
d Stops on Tuesdays to take up for Hull.
e Mondays, Thursdays, and Saturdays. *g* Tuesdays only.

July 1904

HULL and HORNSEA.—L. & N. E.

Miles	Down.	Week Days. mrn	mrn	mrn	mrn	aft (Thursdays and Saturdays.)	aft	aft	aft (Except Saturdays.)	aft	aft	aft	aft (Tues., Thurs., and Sats.)				Sundays. mrn		aft		aft
	Hull (Paragon)...dep.	5 55	8 0	9 46	1158	1 20	2 8	4 15	5 18	6 40	6 33	9 0	10 52	....	....	....	8 23	....	2 23	....	7 43
1	Botanic Gardens	5 59	8 4	9 50	12 2	1 24	2 12	4 19	....	....	6 37	9 4	10 56	....	....	....	8 27	....	2 28	....	7 47
1¾	Stepney	6 2	8 7	9 54	12 6	1 28	2 16	4 22	....	....	6 40	9 7	11 0	....	....	....	8 30	....	2 32	....	7 50
2½	Wilmington †	6 5	8 10	9 57	12 9	1 33	2 19	4 25	b	5 46	6 43	9 10	11 3	....	....	....	8 33	....	2 35	....	7 53
4½	Sutton-on-Hull......	h	8 15	10 2	1214	1 38	2 24	4 30		5 51	6 48	9 15	11 8	....	....	....	8 38	....	2 40	....	7 58
7	Swine	6 16	8 21	10 8	1220	....	2 30	4 36		....	6 54	9 21	11 14	....	....	....	8 44	....	2 46	....	8 4
8¼	Skirlaugh	c	8 25	1012	1224	....	2 34	4 40		....	6.58	9 25	11 18	....	....	....	8 48	....	2 50	....	8 8
9¾	Ellerby	6 24	8 29	1016	1228	....	2 38	4 44		....	7 2	9 29	11 22	....	....	....	8 52	....	2 54	....	8 12
10¾	Whitedale	6 27	8 32	1019	1231	....	2 41	4 47		....	7 5	9 32	11 25	....	....	....	8 55	....	2 57	....	8 15
12¼	Sigglesthorne	6 31	8 36	1023	1235	....	2 45	4 51		....	7 9	9 36	....	....	....	....	8 58	....	3 0	....	8 18
13	Wassand	....	....	....	....	....	....	a		....	....	....	....	....	....	....	....	....	....	....	....
15	Hornsea Bridge	6 36	8 41	1028	1240	1 52	2 50	4 56	n	6 6	7 14	9 41	11 32	....	....	....	....	....	....	....	....
15½	Hornsea ....arr.	6 41	8 46	1033	1245	1 58	2 55	5 1	5 45	6 10	7 18	9 46	11 40	....	....	....	9 9	....	3 13	....	8 28

Miles	Up.	Week Days. mrn	mrn	mrn	mrn	mrn		aft	aft	aft	aft		aft	aft	aft				Sundays. mrn		aft	aft	aft
	Hornsea.........dep.	7 53	8 32	8 50	9 6	10 45	....	1259	3 8	5 13	6 35	....	7 30	8 15	10 0	....	....	....	9 23	....	4 57	8 25	8 44
½	Hornsea Bridge	7 56	8 35	k	9 9	10 48	....	1 2	3 11	5 16	6 38	....	7 33	8 18	10 3	....	....	....	....	....	....	....	....
2½	Wassand	d	....	....	....	....	....	....	....	....	....	....	....	....	....	....	....	....	....	....	....	....	....
3¼	Sigglesthorne	8 2	....	....	9 15	10 54	....	1 8	3 17	....	6 44	....	7 39	....	c	....	....	....	9 31	....	5 5	....	8 52
4¾	Whitedale	8 6	8 42	....	....	10 58	....	1 12	3 21	5 24	....	....	7 43	....	c	....	....	....	9 36	....	5 9	....	8 56
5¾	Ellerby	8 9	....	....	9 20	11 1	....	1 15	3 24	5 27	6 50	....	7 46	....	1015	....	....	....	9 39	....	5 12	8 35	8 59
7¼	Skirlaugh............	8 13	....	....	9 24	11 5	....	1 19	3 28	5 31	6 54	....	k	....	1019	....	....	....	9 43	....	5 16	....	9 3
8¾	Swine................	8 17	....	....	....	11 9	....	1 23	3 32	5 35	....	....	7 54	....	1023	....	....	....	9 47	....	5 20	....	9 7
11	Sutton-on-Hull.......	8 22	8 51	....	9 30	11 14	....	1 28	3 37	5 40	7 1	....	7 59	....	1028	....	....	....	9 52	....	5 25	8 45	9 12
13	Wilmington †	8 28	8 57	....	9 36	11 20	....	1 34	3 43	5 46	7 7	....	8 5	8 38	1034	....	....	....	9 58	....	5 31	8 51	9 18
13¾	Stepney 858.........	8 31	....	....	....	11 23	....	1 37	3 46	5 49	7 10	....	8 8	8 41	1037	....	....	....	10 1	....	5 34	8 54	9 21
14½	Botanic Gardens [878	8 34	9 1	....	....	11 26	....	1 39	3 49	5 52	7 13	....	8 11	8 44	1040	....	....	....	10 3	....	5 36	8 57	9 24
15½	Hull *868,870,874ar	8 38	9 5	9 15	9 41	11 30	....	1 43	3 53	5 56	7 17	....	8 16	8 48	1044	....	....	....	10 8	....	5 41	9 1	9 30

a Stops on Tuesdays to set down from Hull.
b Stops at 5 24 aft. when required to take up.
c Stop when required.
d Stops on Tuesdays to take up for Hull.
h Stops when required to set down.
k Stops when required to take up.
n Stops at 5 43 aft. when required to set down.
* Paragon Station; nearly 1 mile to Cannon Street Station.
† Over ¾ mile to Hull (Cannon Street Station).

July 1924

January 1944

HULL and HORNSEA

Miles		Week Days mrn	mrn	mrn	mrn		aft E	aft S	aft T		aft D	aft	aft	aft		Sundays mrn		aft				
	Hull .... dep	6 10	6 45	7 40	10 3	..	12 5	1252	1 40	..	4 20	5 17	6 20	7 50	..	8 15	..	7 10	..	..	..	..
1	Botanic Gardens...........	..	6 49	7 44	10 7	..	12 9	1256	1 44	..	4 24	5 21	6 24	7 54	..	8 19	..	7 14	..	..	..	..
1¾	Stepney..................	6 15	6 53	7 48	1010	..	1212	1259	1 48	..	4 28	5 25	6 27	7 58	..	8 22	..	7 17	..	..	..	..
2½	Wilmington...............	..	6 58	7 51	1013	..	1215	1 2	1 51	..	4 32	5 29	6 31	8 4	..	8 25	..	7 20	..	..	..	..
4½	Sutton-on-Hull............	6 21	7 3	7 56	1018	..	1220	1 7	1 56	..	4 38	5 35	6 36	8 9	..	8 30	..	7 25	..	..	..	..
7	Swine....................	6 27	7 9	8 1	..	..	1225	1 12	2 2	..	4 43	5 40	6 41	8 14	..	8 35	..	7 30	..	..	..	..
8¼	Skirlaugh	6 31	7 13	8 5	..	..	..	..	2 6	..	4 47	5 44	6 45	8 18	..	..	..	7 34	..	..	..	..
9¾	Ellerby...................	..	7 17	8 9	1027	..	1231	1 18	2 10	..	4 52	5 50	6 49	8 22	..	8 41	..	7 38	..	..	..	..
10¾	Whitedale................	6 37	7 20	8 12	..	..	1234	1 21	2 13	..	4 55	5 54	6 52	8 26	..	8 44	..	7 41	..	..	..	..
12¼	Sigglesthorne	6 41	7 24	8 16	..	..	1238	1 25	2 19	..	4 59	5 58	6 57	8 30	..	8 48	..	7 46	..	..	..	..
15	Hornsea Bridge...........	6 49	7 29	8 27	1036	..	1246	1 33	2 25	..	5 8	6 6	7 5	8 37	..	8 59	..	7 55	..	..	..	..
15½	**Hornsea** .... arr	6 51	7 32	8 29	1038	..	1248	1 35	2 27	..	5 10	6 8	7 7	8 39	..	9 1	..	7 58	..	..	..	..

Miles		Week Days mrn	mrn	mrn	mrn	mrn H		aft E	aft S	aft T	aft	aft	aft	aft		Sundays mrn		aft				
	Hornsea.............. dep	7 10	7 50	8 27	8 56	1055	..	1 5	1 50	2 45	5 25	6 35	7 25	8 55	..	9 17	..	8 15	..	..	..	..
½	Hornsea Bridge...........	7 13	7 53	8 30	8 59	1058	..	1 8	1 53	2 48	5 28	6 38	7 28	8 58	..	9 20	..	8 18	..	..	..	..
3¼	Sigglesthorne	..	7 59	8 35	9 4	11 3	..	1 13	1 58	2 54	5 33	6 43	7 33	9 3	..	9 25	..	8 23	..	..	..	..
4¾	Whitedale................	..	8 3	..	..	11 7	..	1 17	2 2	2 58	5 37	..	7 37	9 7	..	9 29	..	8 27	..	..	..	..
5¾	Ellerby..................	7 23	8 6	8 40	9 9	1110	..	1 21	2 5	3 1	5 40	6 49	7 40	9 10	..	9 32	..	8 30	..	..	..	..
7¼	Skirlaugh	..	8 11	..	..	1114	..	1 25	2 9	3 6	5 44	6 53	..	9 15	..	..	..	8 34	..	..	..	..
8½	Swine....................	..	8 15	..	..	1118	..	1 29	2 13	3 10	5 48	..	7 43	9 20	..	9 38	..	8 38	..	..	..	..
11	Sutton-on-Hull............	7 33	8 21	8 49	9 18	1123	..	1 35	2 18	3 16	5 54	7 2	7 52	9 25	..	9 43	..	8 44	..	..	..	..
13	Wilmington	7 39	8 26	8 54	9 23	1128	..	1 40	2 23	3 21	6 0	7 7	7 57	9 30	..	9 48	..	8 49	..	..	..	..
13¾	Stepney...................	7 42	8 29	8 57	..	1131	..	1 44	2 26	3 24	6 4	7 10	8 1	9 34	..	9 51	..	8 53	..	..	..	..
14½	Botanic Gardens..........	7 45	8 33	9 1	..	1134	..	1 48	2 29	3 28	6 8	7 14	8 5	9 38	..	9 54	..	8 57	..	..	..	..
15½	**Hull**.................. arr	7 50	8 37	9 5	9 28	1138	..	1 52	2 33	3 32	6 12	7 19	8 9	9 42	..	9 58	..	9 1	..	..	..	..

D On Mondays calls at **Wassand** (between Sigglesthorne and Hornsea Bridge) to set down from Hull.
E Except Saturdays. **H** On Mondays calls at **Wassand** (between Hornsea Bridge and Sigglesthorne) to take up for Hull.
S Saturdays only. **T** Thursdays and Saturdays.

HULL and WITHERNSEA.—North Eastern.

Down. Paragon Station,	mrn	mrn	mrn	mrn	aft	aft	aft (Sats. only.)	aft	aft (Tuesdays only.)	aft	aft	aft	aft	aft	aft	aft	Sundays. mrn	aft	aft	
Hull........dep.	5 47	623	....	9 37	12 2	1c8	1 50	2 0	3 6	430	5 8	535	618	723	9 5	1055	7 45	2 15	7 15	....
Botanic Gardens	5 51	637	9b32	9 41	12 6	1c12	....	2 4	310	434	...	...	622	...	9 9	1059	7 49	2 19	7 19	....
Stepney	5 54	640	9b35	9 44	1 9	1c15	1 56	2 7	313	437	...	...	625	728	9 12	11 2	7 52	2 22	7 22	....
Sculcoates	5 57	...	9b38	9 47	1772	....	....	210	316	440	...	...	628	...	9 15	....	7 55	2 25	7 25	....
Southcoates	6 2	645	9b42	9 51	1216	1c20	2 1	214	320	444	515	543	632	733	9 19	11 7	7 59	2 29	7 29	....
Marfleet	6 7	650	....	9 56	1221	....	....	219	325	449	...	...	637	...	9 24	1112	8 4	2 34	7 34	....
Hedon	6 13	658	9b52	10 3	1228	1c29	2 8	226	332	456	...	552	643	742	9 31	1119	8 11	2 41	7 41	....
Rye Hill	6 19	7 3	....	10 9	1234	....		232	338	5 2	...	...	649	748	9 37	1125	8 17	2 47	7 47	....
Keyingham	6 24	7 8	....	1014	1239	....		237	343	5 7	...	6 0	654	753	9 42	1130	8 22	2 52	7 52	....
Ottringham	6 28	713	10b1	1018	1243	1c39		241	347	511	...	6 4	658	757	9 46	1134	8 26	2 56	7 56	....
Patrington	6 34	719	....	1024	1249	....		247	353	517	...	610	7 4	8 3	9 52	1140	8 32	3 2	8 2	....
Withernsea ......arr.	6 43	729	10b15	1035	1258	1c54	2 33	257	4 3	528	545	620	714	813	10 3	1150	8 42	3 12	8 12	....

Mls	Up.	mrn	mrn	mrn	mrn	mrn	aft	aft	aft	aft	aft	aft	aft	aft		Sundays. mrn	aft	aft	aft
—	**Withernsea** ......dep.	6 57	7 55	8 20	8 48	1055	1 12	3 15	5 50	6 40	7 43	8c15	8 23	1020	....	8 57	5 22	8 30	8 47
3¼	Patrington	7 5	8 3	....	8 56	11 3	1 20	3 23	5 58	6 48	7 51	....	8 31	1028	....	9 5	5 30	8 38	8 55
7	Ottringham	7 12	8 10	....	9 3	1110	1 27	3 30	6 5	6 56	7 58	....	8 37	1035	....	9 12	5 37	....	9 2
8½	Keyingham	7 16	8 14	....	....	1114	1 31	3 34	....	7 0	....	....	....	1039	....	9 16	5 41	....	9 6
10	Rye Hill	7 21	8 19	....	....	1119	1 36	3 39	....	7 5	....	....	8 44	1044	....	9 21	5 46	....	9 11
12¼	Hedon	7 27	8 25	....	9 13	1125	1 42	3 45	6 15	7 11	8 8	....	8 50	1050	....	9 27	5 52	8 53	9 17
15¾	Marfleet	7 34	8 32	....	....	1132	1 49	3 52	6 22	7 18	....	....	8 57	1057	....	9 34	5 59	....	9 24
17¼	Southcoates	7 40	8 37	8 45	9 21	1137	1 54	3 57	6 27	7 23	8 17	8c43	9 2	11 2	....	9 39	6 4	9 3	9 29
18¼	Sculcoates	7 44	8 41	....	....	1141	1 58	4 1	6 31	7 27	....	....	....	....	....	9 43	6 8	9 7	9 33
19¼	Stepney *(above)*	7 47	....	....	....	1144	2 1	4 4	6 34	7 30	8 22	8c48	9 7	11 7	....	9 46	6 11	9 10	9 36
19¾	Botanic Gardens	7 49	8 44	....	....	1146	2 3	4 6	6 36	7 32	8 24	8c50	9 9	11 9	....	9 48	6 13	9 12	9 38
20¾	**Hull 574, 569, 570** arr.	7 55	8 51	8 55	9 32	1152	2 10	4 13	6 44	7 39	8 31	8c57	9 16	1115	....	9 54	6 20	9 19	9 45

b Commences on the 9th instant. *c* Mondays, Thursdays, and Saturdays.

July 1904

HULL and WITHERNSEA.—L. & N. E.

Miles.	Down.	mrn	mrn	mrn		aft	aft	aft (Thursdays and Saturdays.)	aft	aft	aft (Except Saturdays.)	aft		aft	aft	aft (Tues., Thurs., and Sats.)		Sundays. mrn		aft	aft
	Hull (Paragon).....dep.	5 47	7 30	10 5	....	1210	1245	1 8	1 58	4 39	5 23	5 33	....	6 40	9 8	1045	....	8 7	....	2 15	7 15
1	Botanic Gardens	5 51	7 34	1010	....	1214	1249	1 12	2 2	4 43	....	....	....	6 44	9 12	1049	....	8 12	....	2 20	7 19
1¾	Stepney	....	7 37	1015	....	1218	1253	1 16	2 6	4 47	....	....	....	6 47	9 16	1053	....	8 16	....	2 24	7 22
2½	Wilmington †	5 56	....	1018	....	1221	1257	....	2 9	4 50	....	5 39	....	6 50	9 19	....	....	8 19	....	2 27	7 25
3½	Southcoates	....	7 42	1021	....	1224	1 0	1 21	2 12	4 55	5 30	5 42	....	6 53	9 22	1058	....	8 23	....	2 33	7 28
5	Marfleet	....	7 47	1028	....	1229	1 5	....	2 17	5 0		5 47	....	6 58	9 27	11 3	....	8 28	....	2 38	7 33
8½	Hedon	h	7 54	1035	....	1236	1 10	1 30	2 24	5 7		5 54	....	7 5	9 34	1110	....	8 35	....	2 45	7 40
10¾	Rye Hill	....	8 0	1041	....	1242	....	....	2 30	5 13		6 0	....	7 11	9 40	1116	....	8 41	....	2 51	7 46
12¼	Keyingham	....	8 5	1046	....	1247	....	....	2 35	5 18		6 5	....	7 16	9 45	1121	....	8 46	....	2 56	7 51
13¾	Ottringham	6 22	8 9	1050	....	1251	....	1 40	2 39	5 22		6 9	....	7 20	9 49	1125	....	8 50	....	3 0	7 55
17	Patrington	6 28	8 15	1056	....	1257	....	1 46	2 45	5 28		6 15	....	7 26	9 55	1131	....	8 56	....	3 6	8 1
20¾	**Withernsea** ......arr.	6 37	8 25	11 8	....	1 7	....	1 56	2 56	5 39	6 0	6 25	....	7 36	10 5	1141	....	9 8	....	3 21	8 11

Miles.	Up.	mrn	mrn		mrn	mrn	mrn		aft	aft	aft	aft		aft	aft	aft	aft			Sundays. mrn	aft	aft	aft
	Withernsea ......dep.	6 50	7 47	....	8 22	8 45	1125	....	....	1 25	3 15	5 54	....	6 50	7 45	8 5	1020	....	....	9 22	5 16	8 26	8 48
3¾	Patrington	6 57	7 54	....	....	8 52	1132	....	....	1 32	3 22	6 1	....	6 57	....	8 12	1027	....	....	9 29	5 23	8 34	8 56
7	Ottringham	7 4	8 1	....	....	8 59	1139	....	....	1 39	3 29	6 8	....	7 4	....	8 19	1034	....	....	9 36	5 30	....	9 3
8½	Keyingham	7 8	8 5	....	....	9 3	1143	....	....	1 43	3 33	6 12	....	7 8	....	8 23	1038	....	....	9 40	5 34	....	9 7
10	Rye Hill	7 13	8 11	....	....	9 8	1148	....	....	1 48	3 38	6 17	....	7 13	....	8 28	1043	....	....	9 45	5 39	....	9 12
12¼	Hedon	7 19	8 18	....	....	9 15	1154	....	1 28	1 54	3 44	6 23	....	7 19	....	8 34	1049	....	....	9 51	5 45	8 50	9 19
15¾	Marfleet	7 26	8 25	....	....	....	12 1	....	1 34	2 1	3 51	6 30	....	7 26	....	c	c	....	....	9 58	5 52	....	9 26
17¼	Southcoates	7 31	8 31	....	8 49	9 26	12 7	....	1 39	2 6	3 56	6 35	....	7 31	8 14	8 46	11 1	....	....	10 3	5 57	9 2	9 33
18¼	Wilmington †	7 35	8 35	....	....	....	1211	....	1 43	2 10	4 0	6 39	....	7 35	....	8 50	....	....	....	10 7	6 1	9 6	9 37
19	Stepney 859	7 38	8 38	....	....	....	1215	....	1 46	2 13	4 3	6 42	....	7 38	8 19	8 53	11 6	....	....	1010	6 4	9 10	9 40
19¾	Botanic Gardens...878	7 41	8 41	....	....	....	1218	....	1 49	2 16	4 6	6 45	....	7 40	8 22	8 56	11 9	....	....	1012	6 6	9 13	9 42
20¾	**Hull*868, 870, 874**, arr.	7 45	8 45	....	8 56	9 34	1222	....	1 53	2 20	4 10	6 49	....	7 44	8 26	9 0	1113	....	....	1017	6 12	9 17	9 48

c Stop when required.
h Stops when required to set down.
* Paragon; nearly 1 mile to Cannon Street Station.
† Over ¾ mile to Hull (Cannon Street) Station.

July 1924

January 1944

HULL and WITHERNSEA

Miles		Week Days mrn	mrn	mrn		aft E	aft S	aft E	aft S		aft	aft	aft	aft		Sundays mrn		aft				
	Hull........dep	5 25	6 30	7 30	..	1211	1240	1 30	2 0	..	4 35	5 25	6 5	7 40	..	8 5	..	7 5	..	..	..	..
1	Botanic Gardens........	5 29	6 34	7 34	..	1215	1244	1 34	2 4	..	4 39	..	6 9	7 44	..	8 9	..	7 9	..	..	..	..
1¾	Stepney........	..	6 38	7 38	..	1218	1247	1 38	2 8	..	4 43	..	6 14	7 48	..	8 12	..	7 12	..	..	..	..
2½	Wilmington........	5 35	6 43	..	..	1221	1250	1 43	2 13	..	4 47	5 33	6 19	7 54	..	8 15	..	7 15	..	..	..	..
3½	Southcoates........	..	6 47	7 44	..	1224	1254	1 47	2 17	..	4 51	5 38	6 25	7 58	..	8 18	..	7 18	..	..	..	..
5¼	Marfleet........	..	6 52	7 49	..	1229	1259	1 52	2 22	..	4 56	5 44	6 31	8 3	..	8 23	..	7 23	..	..	..	..
8¼	Hedon........	5 46	6 58	7 55	..	1235	1 5	1 59	2 28	..	5 3	5 51	6 37	8 10	..	8 30	..	7 29	..	..	..	..
10¾	Rye Hill and Burstwick..	..	7 5	8 2	..	1242	1 11	2 6	2 35	..	5 10	5 58	6 45	8 17	..	8 36	..	7 35	..	..	..	..
12½	Keyingham........	..	7 10	8 7	..	1246	1 15	2 11	2 40	..	5 14	6 4	6 50	8 23	..	8 41	..	7 39	..	..	..	..
14	Ottringham........	6 3	7 15	8 12	..	1250	1 19	2 15	2 44	..	5 19	6 9	6 55	8 29	..	8 45	..	7 43	..	..	..	..
17	Patrington........	6 9	7 21	8 18	..	1256	1 25	2 22	2 51	..	5 25	6 15	7 1	8 35	..	8 52	..	7 50	..	..	..	..
20¾	Withernsea........arr	6 18	7 31	8 28	..	1 7	1 36	2 32	3 1	..	5 36	6 26	7 12	8 46	..	9 1	..	8 0	..	..	..	..

Miles		Week Days mrn	mrn	mrn	mrn		aft E	aft S	aft		aft	aft	aft			Sundays mrn		aft				
	Withernsea........dep	6 45	7 53	8 18	8 48	..	1 23	1 55	4 17	..	6 35	7 30	9 5	..	..	9 15	..	8 20	..	..	..	..
3¼	Patrington........	6 52	8 0	..	8 55	..	1 30	2 2	4 24	..	6 42	7 37	9 12	..	..	9 23	..	8 27	..	..	..	..
6¾	Ottringham........	6 59	8 7	..	9 1	..	1 37	2 9	4 30	..	6 52	7 43	9 19	..	..	9 30	..	8 33	..	..	..	..
8¼	Keyingham........	7 4	8 11	..	9 5	..	1 41	2 13	4 34	..	6 58	7 48	9 23	..	..	9 34	..	8 37	..	..	..	..
10	Rye Hill and Burstwick....	7 8	8 16	..	9 10	..	1 45	2 17	4 39	..	7 4	7 53	9 28	..	..	9 38	..	8 41	..	..	..	..
12½	Hedon........	7 14	8 23	..	9 17	..	1 52	2 23	4 46	..	7 10	7 59	9 34	..	..	9 44	..	8 47	..	..	..	..
15½	Marfleet........	7 21	8 30	..	..	..	1 58	2 29	4 52	..	7 16	8 5	9 40	..	..	9 51	..	8 54	..	..	..	..
17¼	Southcoates........	7 27	8 37	8 46	9 26	..	2 4	2 34	4 58	..	7 22	8 11	9 45	..	..	9 56	..	9 0	..	..	..	..
18¼	Wilmington........	7 31	8 40	8 49	..	..	2 7	2 37	5 1	..	7 25	8 14	9 49	..	..	10 0	..	9 4	..	..	..	..
19	Stepney........	7 34	8 43	..	..	..	2 10	2 41	5 4	..	7 28	8 17	9 53	..	..	10 3	..	9 8	..	..	..	..
19¾	Botanic Gardens........	7 37	8 47	..	..	..	2 14	2 45	5 8	..	7 31	8 20	9 57	..	..	10 6	..	9 12	..	..	..	..
20¾	Hull........arr	7 41	8 51	8 57	9 35	..	2 19	2 50	5 12	..	7 35	8 24	10 1	..	..	1010	..	9 16	..	..	..	..

E Except Saturdays. **S** Saturdays only.

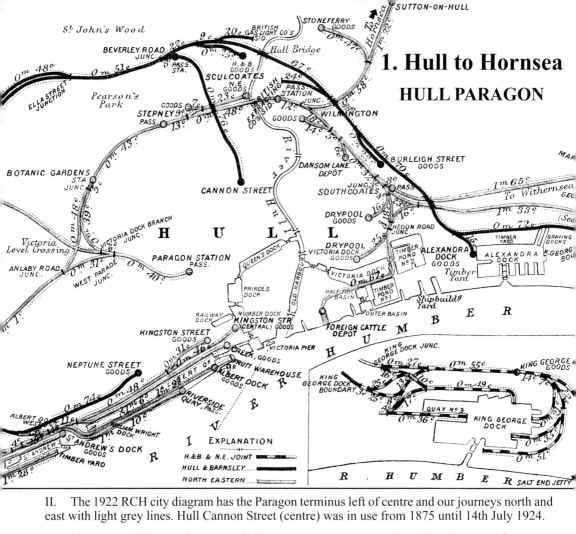

1. Hull to Hornsea
HULL PARAGON

II.   The 1922 RCH city diagram has the Paragon terminus left of centre and our journeys north and east with light grey lines. Hull Cannon Street (centre) was in use from 1875 until 14th July 1924.

III.   The 1929 edition at 6ins to 1 mile has Paragon Square on the right, plus part of Paragon Street from which the station took its name. The northern part of the station had been created in 1901-02 by demolishing houses on the southern side of Colliers Street. On the left is West Parade Junction. Its 120-lever signal box worked from 1903 to 29th March 1980. The first Paragon Box lasted from 1875 to 1904 and had 33 levers. The second was used until 1938 and had a 143-lever power frame. They were east of the bridge. There were also two boxes working the same dates and named Park Street. Their frames took 46 and 179 levers, respectively, and were both west of Park Street.

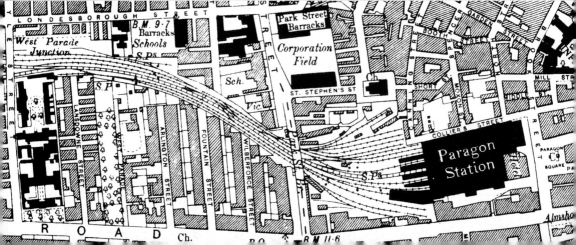

1.   The fine station complex came into use in 1848 and both railways used it. Connections to the two new branches on which we travel followed in the early 1860s, although the southern one terminated at Victoria Dock until 1864. The hotel is on the left and its extent is shown on map III. (R.Humm coll.)

HULL

2.   This class A6 4-6-2T has lost its LNER letters, but it gained its BR number, which is 69796. It was recorded on 25th March 1949, bound for Withernsea, and is coupled to an elderly main line coach. (W.A.Camwell/SLS)

3.   The suffix 'Paragon' was little used after 1939. The porte-cochere and clock seen in picture 1 were removed in the early 1960s to make way for the offices seen in picture 7. The three telephone boxes are painted cream. Hull Corporation Telephones was the only UK municipal-owned telephone company. (R.Humm coll.)

4.   In World War I, on 5th March 1916, a Zeppelin raid killed 17 and the bomb blast blew out the glass in the station roof. Seen in 1957 is class G5 0-4-4T no. 67263, which was ex-NER. It has an insulated van between it and the passenger coach for the speedy conveyance of cold fish or meat. The nearest roofing is part of the original station of 1848. (Colour-Rail.com)

5.   The five spans over the platforms and the two-span roof over the concourse were completed by 1908. Part of the hotel became offices. Platforms 1 to 9 had received low level roofing by December 1904. (Colour-Rail.com)

6.　In 1904, the station signalling system was converted to electro-pneumatic power signalling. The station had two signal boxes: Paragon Station was a 143-lever box, located at the end of platforms 1 and 2, and Park Street box, with 179 levers, was located west of the station. This westward view is from 21st August 1964 and includes the 1938 signal box, beyond the left end of the long span of Park Street Bridge. This was built in 1871 and was the first of many to replace level crossings in the area. The box had a small panel initially and a large one from 1984. (Colour-Rail.com)

7.　Paragon House was built in 1962 and replaced the entrance canopy. It became the regional headquarters for BR and was demolished in 2006. (D.A.Thompson)

BOTANIC GARDENS

IV. The tracks lower right overlap those on the previous map and trains on our two branches all used the curve marked VICTORIA DOCK BRANCH. The engine shed close to it came into use in 1901, when the one near to the terminus closed. The station is further north. The orphanage was for the benefit of the children of Hull's seamen who had died. On 14th February 1927, Argyle Street Bridge was the site of a head-on train collision, caused by a signalling error, in which 12 passengers were killed and 24 seriously injured.

8.   A tram rumbles north along Princes Avenue after 1900, when they started running here. The bracket on the nearest pole carried two supply wires, but they are not visible. (LOSA)

For details of the trams, see *Hull Tramways*, a Middleton Press album packed with local history. The same applies to *Hull Trolleybuses*.

Bradshaw, December 1895

9.　Hull Botanical Gardens was created nearby in 1812 and moved to the site of what was to be Hymers College in 1889. The station opened on 1st June 1853 and was originally known as Hull Cemetery. It closed to passengers in November 1854, before being reopened as Hull Cemetery Gates in September 1866. It was renamed Hull Botanic Gardens on 1st November 1881, as was the 20-lever signal box. It had 39 from 8th October 1900, as electric trams would cross here. There was provision for a four-lever 'Tram Frame' to work tram signals and trap points. On 24th July 1937, electric trams ceased to cross the railway here. The box closed on 26th October 1968. (P.Laming coll.)

10.　The station closed on 19th October 1964 and was demolished in 1976, to be replaced by a public house called 'Old Zoological', in November 1994. The signals are for the branch to the terminus and the wicket gates were for local people and hand carts. Average data from 1927 showed the gates across the road closed 101 times daily, for a total of 4 hours 13 minutes. (Stations UK)

HULL (Kingston-upon-Hull).

Bradshaw's Guide, 1866.

Telegraph stations at Nos. 37, 52, and 53, Lowgate, 6, Minerva Place, Quay Side, and Railway stations.

HOTELS.—Royal Station Hotel, for families, private or commercial gentlemen ; The George ; Glover's Commercial Hotel ; Vittoria Hotel on the Quay.

POST HORSES, FLYS, &c., at the hotels. Tariff— 1s. 6d. per mile. 1s. from any railway station to the town.

MARKET DAYS——Tuesday and Friday.

PLACES OF RESORT, &c., IN HULL.

The BOTANICAL GARDENS are on the Anlaby Road. An agreeable resort to the pleasure-seeker and practical botanist. Admission by order from subscribers.

QUEEN'S THEATRE, Paragon Street.

The LITERARY and PHILOSOPHICAL SOCIETY'S MUSEUM—ROYAL INSTITUTION, Albion Street. Admission by orders from any of the directors or subscribers.

The MUSEUM of the MECHANICS' INSTITUTE may be viewed on application to the Librarian at the Institute, George Street.

Mr. SEAMEN'S MUSUEM is at that gentleman's residence, near the Cemetery, and contains many valuable natural curiosities.

MISCELLANEOUS SOCIETIES.–Amongst the societies designed to improve the social condition of the people, may be noticed the Hull Temperance League ; the Hull Auxiliary Peace Society, W. Morley, Esq., President ; and the Vocal Society— Conductor, Mr Skelton.

This parliamentary borough and old town, founded by Edward I., as a King's Town, or Kingston-upon-Hull (which is still its official name), stands on the *Yorkshire* side of the Humber, in a very flat and uninviting spot, but admirably fitted for trade, which has much augmented in the last few years. Population, 97,661, who send two members. The river Humber, the main estuary into which the Ouse and the Yorkshire streams, with the Trent, all four flow, is here 2 miles broad, and widens to 5 or 6 before it joins the sea at Spurn Head, which is 20 miles below. All this coast of the East Riding is in progress of change—the sea gaining on the shores of the north sea, where Ravenspur, Potterfleet, and other ports, once in existence, have been swallowed up, while it is retiring, if anything, on the Hull shore, where Sunk Island (towards Spurn Head), which

first appeared above water in 1630, is now a fertile cultivated tract of 4,500 acres in extent. So flat is the country that the railway to Selby westward, though 31 miles long, runs for the most part on a made embankment, and has neither tunnel nor viaduct. The loss of the ancient sea ports of the Riding led to the foundation of Hull.

Brick clay is abundant, and Hull has several specimens of *very old* brick buildings. The *Citadel* with its old moated fortress contained the barracks and magazines, and stood two sieges in the civil war ; the first being in 1642, when the refusal of Sir J. Hotham, the Governor, to deliver the town to Charles I., who appeared in person before it, was the first act of hostility between the King and Parliament. Hotham in the next year proving treacherous, was executed at Tower Hill. A bridge of three arches crosses the Hull in the middle of the town, near the upper entrance of the *Docks*, which form a loop with it and the Humber, and contain 30 acres, besides two basins of 3 acres more. *Queen's Dock*, cut in 1778, contains 13 acres, and is 1,700 feet by 254 feet ; the others are the *Humber's Prince, Railway,* and *Victoria Docks,* and all surrounded by large warehouses. and timber yards. Upwards of 100,000 tons of shipping are owned by the port ; and the customs duties amount to nearly half a million. Pottery, bricks, white lead, soap, oil-cake, rope, sails, grain, timber, iron—figure among the articles of trade. Many seamen are engaged in the Greenland whale fisheries and Baltic trade. Fox, who attempted the north-west passage up Fox's Channel, and perished in 1586, Johnson the botanist, Spence the entomologist, and B. Thompson, and his brother were natives.

Among the buildings are the *Public Rooms*, built in 1830, having a hall 90 feet long. Large parish *Church of Trinity,* in the Market Place, built in 1312, one of the largest in the kingdom, in the shape of a Gothic cross, 270 feet long and 170 feet through the *early brick transept* ; steeple, 150 feet high ; and a fine organ, by Foster and Andrews, *Wilberforce Column,* near the Prince's Bridge, founded in his honour, on the 1st August, 1834 (the day of negro emancipation), 80 feet high. Wilberforce was born at Hull, in 1759, and died in 1853, but not till he had the happiness of knowing that the bill was safe, and that the great work of his useful life was achieved. "Thank God (he said), that I have lived to see the day when an English parliament is willing to give 20 millions to abolish slavery."

Mls	Down.	mrn	mrn	mrn	aft		aft	aft	aft	aft	Sndys		Up.	mrn	mrn	mrn	aft	aft	aft	aft	mrn	aft
—	Hull (ParagnSta)	6 45	7 45	9 45	2 5		3 38	4 20	5 47	8 55	8 5		Hornsea....dep	8 0	9 0	10 50	3 15	5 25	6 45	9 55	9 25	5 30
1	Botanic Gardens	6 49	7 49	9 49	2 9		3 42			8 59	8 9		Hornsea Bridge.	8 3	9 2	10 53	3 18		6 48		9 28	...
1¼	Stepney	6 52	7 52	9 52	2 12	3 45		5 51	9	8 12		Goxhill	c								
2¼	Sculcoates	6 55		9 55	2 15	3 48			9	8 15		Sigglesthorne ..	8 9	d	10 59	3 24		6 54	10 1	9 34	5 37
2¼	Wilmington	6 58	7 56	9 58	2 18	3 53	4 32	5 54	9	8 18	4 30	Whitedale	8 13		11 3	3 28		6 58	10 5	9 38	5 41
4¼	Sutton-on-Hull	7 3	8 1	10 3	2 23	3 58	4 37	5 59	9 13	8 23	4 35	Burton Constble	8 16	9 12	11 6	3 31	5 35	7 1	10 8	9 41	5 44
7	Swine	7 9		10 9	2 29	4 4		6 5	9 19	8 29	4 41	Ellerby	c								
8¼	Skirlaugh	7 13		10 13	2 33	4 8		6 9	9 23	8 33	4 45	Skirlaugh	8 20		11 10	3 35		7	5 10	12 9	9 45	5 48
9	Ellerby				a							Swine	8 24		11 14	3 39	5 42	7	9 10	15 9	9 49	5 52
9¼	Burton Constble	7 17	8 14	10 17	2 37	4 15	4 47	6 13	9 27	8 37	4 49	Sutton-on-Hull	8 30	9 21	11 20	3 45	5 48	7 15	10 20	9 55	5 58
10½	Whitedale	7 20		10 20	2 40	4 18		6 16	9 30	8 40	4 52	Wilmington	8 35	9 26	11 25	3 50	5 54	7 20	10 25	10 0	6 3
13½	Sigglesthorne	7 24		10 24	2 44	4 22	b	6 20	9 34	8 44	4 58	Sculcoates	8 37		11 27	3 52		7 22			6 5
14¼	Goxhill				a							Stepney	8 40		11 30	3 55	5 58	7 25	10 28		6 8
15	Hornsea Bridge	7 33	8 25	10 33	2 53	4 32	4 57	6 28	9 43	8 53		Botanic Gardens	8 43		11 33	3 58	6 1	7 28	10 31		6 11
15¼	Hornsea....arr	7 35	8 27	10 35	2 55	4 35	5 0	6 30	9 45	8 56	5 7	Hull 260, 271 a	8 50	9 36	11 40	4 56	10	7 37	10 40		6 20

a Stops to set down from Hull.   *b* Stops to set down 1st class Passengers from Hull and Stations beyond.   *c* Stops on Tuesdays to take up for Hull.   *d* Stops to take up 1st class Passengers for Hull and Stations beyond.

11.   Beyond the left fence is the goods yard, which closed on 6th September 1965. The signalman waits while a crowd is dealt with on 28th May 1955. Blowing off is class 3 2-6-2T no. 40059, which is heading the 5.30pm from Hornsea. Part of the signal box is lower left. The gateman is lower right. He used a red flag to control road traffic. (SLS coll.)

12.   This view from the footbridge is from 10th October 1964, only nine days before closure. The 'Cats Whiskers' had long been covered by a bright yellow panel to improve sighting by track workers. (Colour-Rail.com)

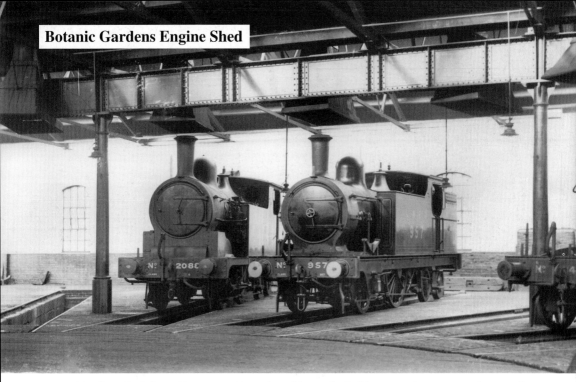

13.   Of the four sheds in Hull to enter BR service, this one had a bias towards passenger locomotives. It is seen on 21st June 1931, with class G5 0-4-4T no. 2088 and class X2 2-2-4T no. 957, at rest. The latter spent most of its time here, hauling an officers saloon. (H.C.Casserley)

14.   On the left on the same day is one of the Sentinel railcars introduced by the LNER in the mid-1920s, but seldom used on the routes of this album. Centre is class Y8 0-4-0T no. 559, built in 1890, and behind it is a Sentinel vertical boilered 0-4-0T, a type produced in 1925-31. (H.C.Casserley)

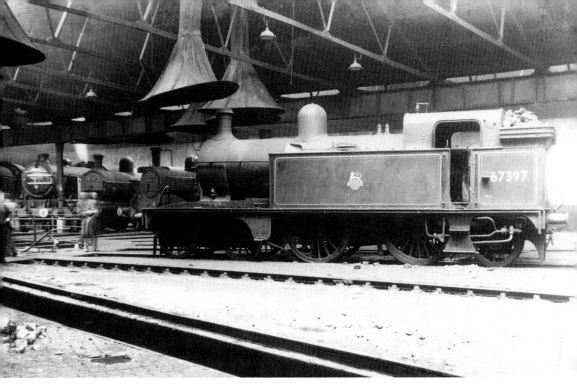

15.   No. 67397 was a class C12 4-4-2T and was photographed on 24th August 1952. The shed had two turntables in it and was coded 53B. (R.M.Casserley)

From *Good Lines*, monthly journal of the Temperance Society, dated 1911.

16.   The shed closed to steam traction in June 1959. A mechanical coaling plant had been installed in 1932, but the early coal stage building is the main structure in this view from 26th August 1958. It was used by railcars to their end. On the left is the water tank. (Colour-Rail.com)

17.   The shed was rebuilt in the mid-1950s to accommodate DMUs and a few diesel shunters. This is the scene on 13th October 1963, but most items have vanished. Listed in 2008 were sidings for tampers, washing and fuelling. Five carriage sidings were south of the seven platforms of Hull terminus. (R.S.Carpenter)

V. The 1911 edition at 6ins to 1 mile has Sculcoates station close to the bridge at the right border. It was closed from 1854 to 1865 and then permanently from 9th June 1912, but its signal box closed in 1907. The Car Depot in the centre was Hull Tramway's track store. It had access to the adjacent goods yard. The goods shed is on the right and Stepney station is on the left. It opened with the line, but had a closure period from 1854 to 1864. Trams used the level crossing close to the station from 8th December 1900 to 3rd September 1938. Their tracks are not shown at this scale.

18. We look west from Beverley Road level crossing. Unclear in the distance is the gate box by the level crossing over Park Road. The long building, left of centre, was a saw mill. Park Road Gate Box was originally called Terry Street. It had two gate wheels and five levers. On 15th June 1943, a replacement locking frame and two gate wheels came into use, but on 26th October 1968 all was closed. (Stations UK)

19. Sanitary history can be found on the right, where there is roofless provision for gentlemen, near the barrow. The low brick wall was a late addition, so that users could not be seen leaving, adjusting their clothes. The main building is listed Grade II. (R.Humm coll.)

20. A coal concentration depot was established here on 11th July 1960, but all goods traffic ceased on 6th September 1965. A 30cwt crane had been provided. The connection to the goods yard and the tramway store is in the background. The signal box was in use from about 1900 to 1968. (R.Humm coll.)

21. Running in on 24th June 1956 is class V3 2-6-2T no. 67663 with compartment coaches forming the 6.0pm from Withernsea. The station became unstaffed on 4th January 1960. Goods trains passed through until 1968, but there were no passenger services here after 19th October 1964. (SLS coll.)

22. Eastbound in the early 1960s is a DMU acting as the ultimate observation car, before all drivers chose to have the blinds down behind them, always. The dwellings near the rear of the train could only be accessed from Cave Street. (R.Humm coll.)

← VI. Our route is the lower one on the left border and the Hornsea line is marked on the right. On it is Stoneferry Junction Signal Box, which opened in about 1913 and had 26 levers. The Withernsea line diverges south from it at Wilmington Junction. The map is dated 1947 and it shows a long siding curving west to the oil refinery of the British Extracting Works. Its embankment had carried no track on the 1911 edition; see map VII. The two lines lower right continue on the top of map XX featuring Southcoates, prior to picture no. 65. The Hornsea branch and the Alexandra Dock line were linked by a curve from 1969 to 1976. Above centre is the 1915 branch with sidings to the River Hull. Their closure also came in 1976, although an oil refinery is shown being served. Black circles and rectangles represent the Bankside Gas Works of the British Gas Light Company. It supplied most of Hull with coal gas until 1960. Naptha and LPG were then used until closure in 1973. 104,837 tons of coal were received in 1913, mostly by rail, and 81,771 tons in 1947, plus 1,900,000 gallons of oil. Many consumers were lost during WWII.

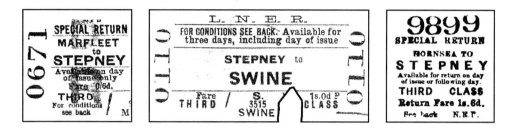

23.   The first swing bridge here over the River Hull carried interlaced tracks and is evident on the left. The first train over the new one was recorded on 5th May 1907; it had double track. (J.Alsop coll.)

24. By the mid-1970s, the building was in terminal decline. The 1907 signal box had been on the south side of the line and was originally called Sculcoates. It was later changed to Wincolmlee; it had 31 levers and a gate wheel. (R.Humm coll.)

25. The bridge was restored by Hull City Council. It is seen on 17th August 2014, when it just carried a footpath. Attention to detail included a life belt, but not the smoke deflectors. The box had just five levers and was not a block post. (R.Humm coll.)

WILMINGTON

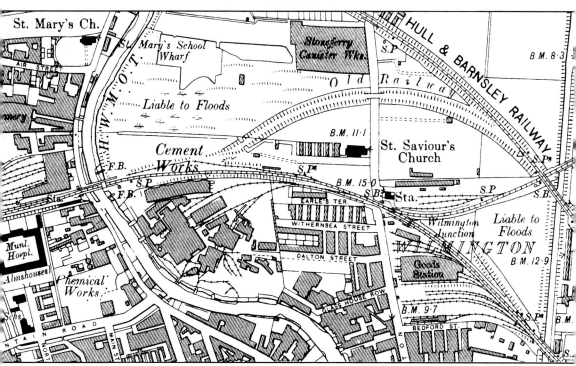

VII. This 1911 edition overlaps map V on the left and includes the entire embankment of the abandoned connection. The platforms are easier to see on the next map, but this features the H&BR clearly.

26. A single island platform came into use on 9th June 1912 and it was positioned nearer to the swing bridge, which is in the distance. Thus this gave access to trains on both branches and can be seen on map VI. The tall building on the right was a seed-crushing plant. It went in 2014. (R.Humm coll.)

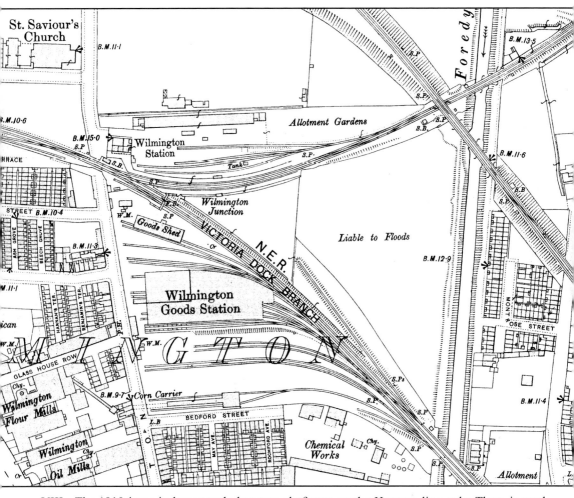

VIII. The 1910 issue in larger scale has two platforms on the Hornsea line only. There is road access to the down one, but a footbridge is shown to the up one. The goods yard had a 5-ton crane listed in 1938.

Wilmington East Box diagram from 1914. Closure came on 2nd January 1960.

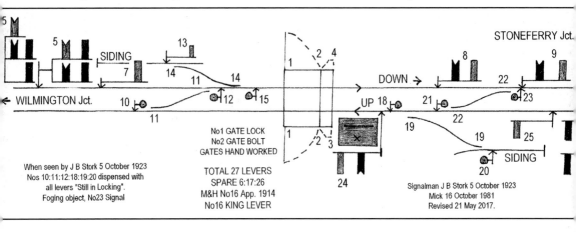

STONEFERRY Jct.

SIDING

WILMINGTON Jct.

DOWN →

UP 18

SIDING

No1 GATE LOCK
No2 GATE BOLT
GATES HAND WORKED

When seen by J B Stork 5 October 1923
Nos 10:11:12:18:19:20 dispensed with
all levers "Still in Locking".
Foging object, No23 Signal

TOTAL 27 LEVERS
SPARE 6:17:26
M&H No16 App. 1914
No16 KING LEVER

Signalman J B Stork 5 October 1923
Mick 16 October 1981
Revised 21 May 2017.

27. This view from July 1961 is in the same direction and reveals the extent of the wooden construction. This was needed due to the soft ground of the valley side. Total closure came on 19th October 1964. (E.Wilmshurst)

28. The final image is in the other direction and shows the access to the subway, which led to Foster Street in later years. The booking office was there and was still evident in 2010. Junction Box is visible on the right; it was in use from 1912 until 1968 and later became a café. It had 50 levers. (Stations UK)

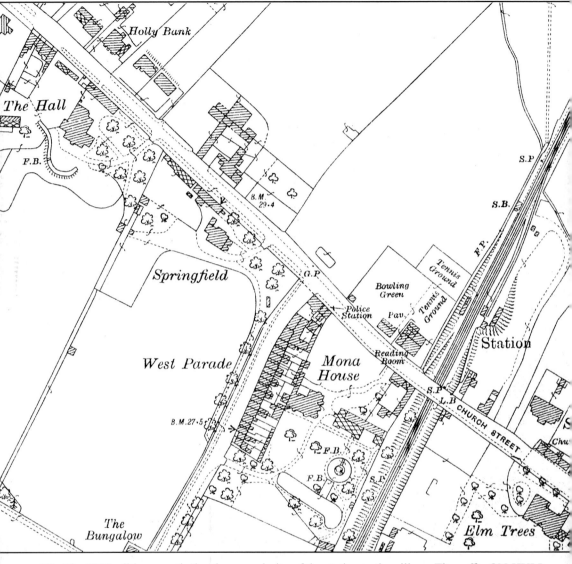

IX. The 1928 edition reveals the close proximity of the station to the village. The suffix ON-HULL was added on 1st December 1874, as there were so many Suttons elsewhere. It means 'South Town'.

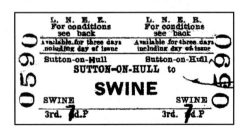

29.   Over bridges were chosen as the ground surface is less than 30ft above sea level. One of the two sloping access paths is visible. The booking office is at the top of it. The staff and some family members were often invited to pose by postcard photographers. (P.Laming coll.)

30.   The spacious house for the station master is featured. Good viewpoints were always chosen, for security reasons. Featured is class J77 0-6-0T no. 1461, together with local coal deliveries in the yard. (J.Alsop coll.)

31. This panorama northwards from the road bridge confirms the level nature of the environs and the limited extent of the goods yard. In the distance is the signal box, which was in use from 1898 to 1964. It had 24 levers. (J.Alsop coll.)

←   32. The fine vista from the bridge includes the station building with its single chimney. The fires would have to heat the booking office, waiting room and staff facilities. Sadly, no details of the special train were found. Closure came on 19th October 1964, but the goods yard was open until 3rd May 1965. The site was cleared and a public footpath created, along with a local playground. (P.Laming coll.)

Bradshaw, February 1887

SWINE

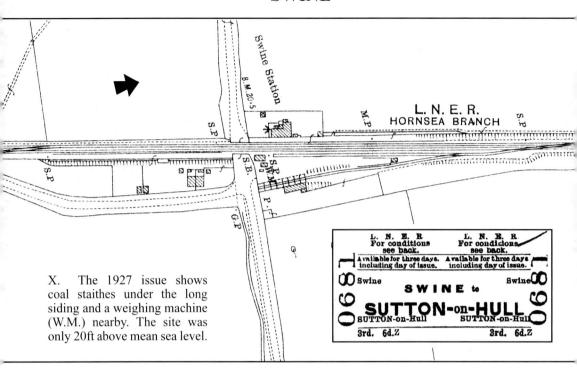

X. The 1927 issue shows coal staithes under the long siding and a weighing machine (W.M.) nearby. The site was only 20ft above mean sea level.

33. An early view north includes all four lamps on the down side. The tiny village was ½ mile to the west. The name perhaps derives from the Old English 'swin', meaning 'creek'. (LOSA)

34. This 1955 illustration reveals the staggered platforms and that the signalman had a wheel to swing all the gates at once. Featured is class L1 2-6-4T no. 67766, with one head lamp visible. Introduced in 1945, the class numbered 100. The box was in use from around 1902 to 1964. It had 29 levers and a gate wheel. (N.Stead/Transport Treasury)

35. This 1962 record shows all structures complete. Although the station had been unstaffed since 4th January 1960, the house was still occupied and remained so. The trackbed became part of the Hornsea Rail Trail. The goods yard closed on 11th November 1963 and passenger carriage ended on 19th October 1964. (Stations UK)

SKIRLAUGH

XI. The 1927 map shows the coal staithes, on the north
side. The inset siding was almost one mile north of the
station. Ellerby West Siding ground frame opened in 1903,
with one gate wheel and nine levers.

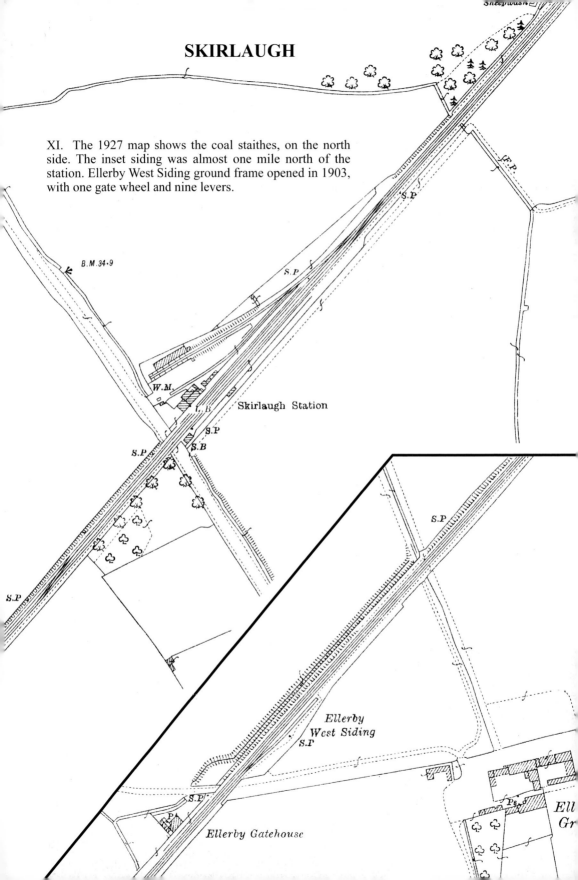

Sheepwash

F.P.

S.P

B.M. 34·9

S.P

S.P

W.M.

L.B

Skirlaugh Station

S.P

S.B

S.P

S.P

S.P

S.P

Ellerby
West Siding
S.P

S.P

P

Ellerby Gatehouse

P

Ell
Gr

36.   Here, the crossing for passengers and luggage was separate from the main one. The lamp on the gate was fitted with red glass, for night safety. (P.Laming coll.)

37.   The station master and his family would be glad to pose for posterity, no doubt. The signalman has a perfect view too. His box was manned from 1902 to 1964 and had 27 levers, plus a gate wheel, initially. Later, there were only seven levers and the gates were worked by hand. (P.Laming coll.)

38. It is 31st August 1956 and alterations are in progress prior to closure on 6th May 1957. The goods yard lasted until 3rd May 1965. (H.C.Casserley)

39. This 1962 panorama is devoid of most lamps and all name boards of course, but the staff accommodation is clear. There had been just a single track on the branch initially, but doubling took place around 1900. (Stations UK)

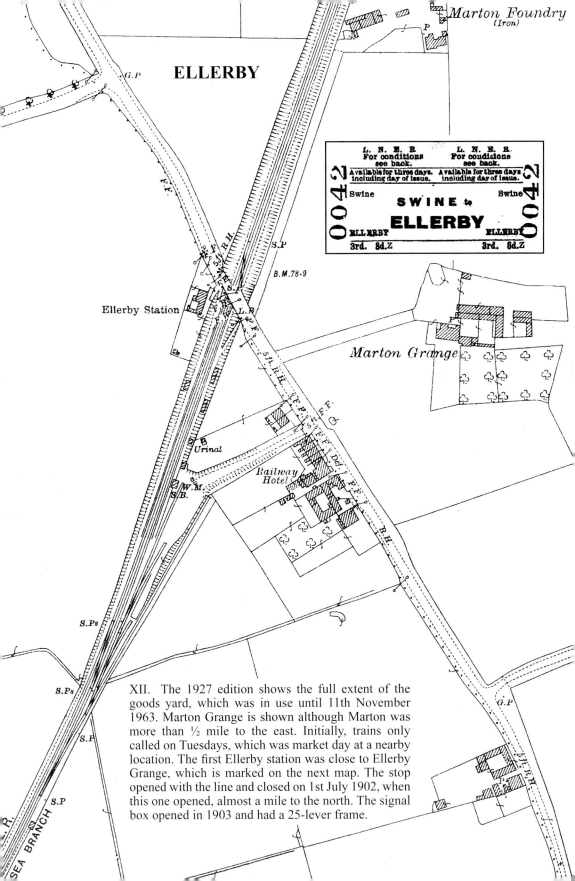

ELLERBY

Marton Foundry (Iron)

G.P

Ellerby Station

B.M.78·9

Marton Grange

Urinal

Railway Hotel

W.M.
S.B.

S.Ps

S.Ps

S.P

S.P

L.R.
SEA BRANCH

G.P

XII. The 1927 edition shows the full extent of the goods yard, which was in use until 11th November 1963. Marton Grange is shown although Marton was more than ½ mile to the east. Initially, trains only called on Tuesdays, which was market day at a nearby location. The first Ellerby station was close to Ellerby Grange, which is marked on the next map. The stop opened with the line and closed on 1st July 1902, when this one opened, almost a mile to the north. The signal box opened in 1903 and had a 25-lever frame.

40. A 1962 panorama gives the passenger's view and the number of chimney pots on the station house. The map includes a urinal, which is to the right of the camera. Staffing ceased on 4th January 1960 when the station became a halt. Closure came on 19th October 1964. (Stations UK)

XIII. The 1947 revision at 1in to 1 mile is included to show the source of the station's second name: Burton Constable. The massive estate is just below centre. It had been Marton for its first five months. The second was used until 1st January 1922. The location of the two Skirlaugh villages can be found top left.

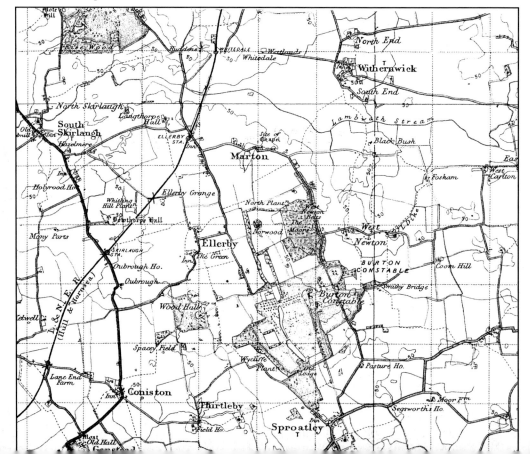

WHITEDALE

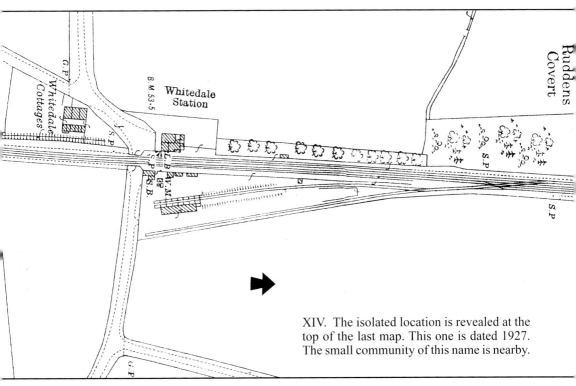

XIV. The isolated location is revealed at the top of the last map. This one is dated 1927. The small community of this name is nearby.

41. The foot crossing to the second platform to arrive is beyond the main crossing. The latter has a wheel evident for the control of its gates. The small window lower right was to illuminate the locking room into which all the lever ends projected. There were 29 levers. They were in use in 1903-64. (J.Alsop coll.)

42. Examination of the frontage in about 1910 will reveal a Royal Mail letter box, which explains L.B on the map. Many signal wires run between the platform edge and the point rods. (LOSA)

43. A 1962 view shows the situation between losing staff on 4th January 1960 and total closure on 19th October 1964. The goods yard had no crane and ceased to be used on 3rd May 1965. (Stations UK)

SIGGLESTHORNE

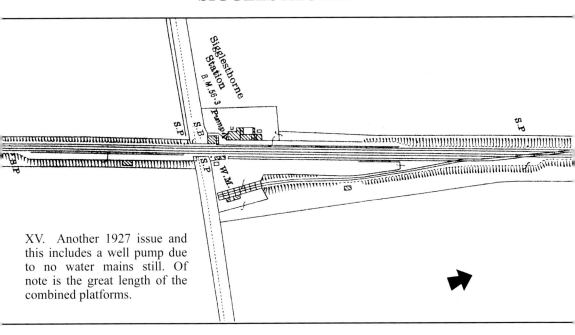

XV. Another 1927 issue and this includes a well pump due to no water mains still. Of note is the great length of the combined platforms.

44. Looking south, we find the chimney of the platelayers cabin on the left and the signalman completing the trio of happy onlookers. A flowerbed brought joy to passengers at many stations. (P.Laming coll.)

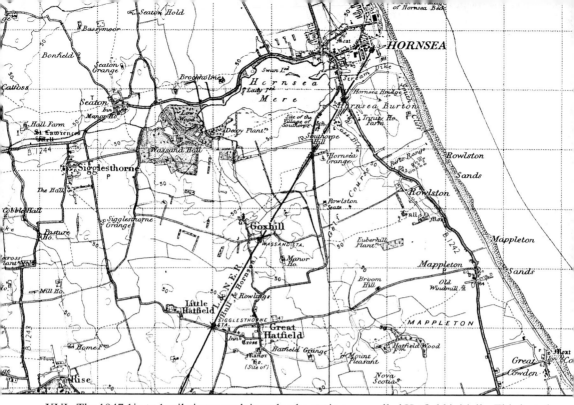

XVI. The 1947 1in to 1 mile issue explains why the station was called Hatfield initially. This lasted until 1st October 1874. There were other Hatfield stations by then. The reason for the station at Goxhill not being so called is evident.

45. Seldom can we enjoy the signalman's pleasure in this way. We can also study the mechanism of the gate wheel, as he had moved on to the lever frame. There had been 29 levers and a gate wheel. Closure came in 1964. (J.Alsop coll.)

46.   It is 31st August 1956; we can assume that Mr Casserley asked to occupy the rear cab of a new DMU. We can see the final style of gate lamp, plus the flat nature of the locality. (H.C.Casserley)

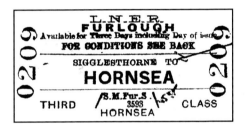

47.   The goods yard had been beyond the small 'gangers hut' and traffic ceased on 11th November 1963. Passengers' movement ended on 19th October 1964 and the property became a pleasant dwelling, with platforms. (Stations UK)

WASSAND

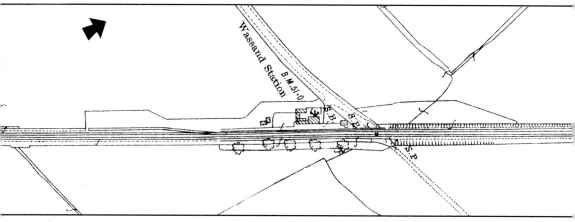

XVII. The station's name was Goxhill until 1st October 1904. The village can be seen on the previous map. This one was issued in 1927. The name was changed, due to it being duplicated in Lincolnshire.

➜ 48. For most of its life, the station only received one train each way per week. It was on Mondays, the nearest market day. No goods service was listed in 1938, but it officially ceased on 31st October 1960. (P.Laming coll.)

49. A 1962 view from the level crossing reveals a clearance of the usual details, as the last passenger train had called in September 1953. The house avoided demolition; the single point rod is still in place. (Stations UK)

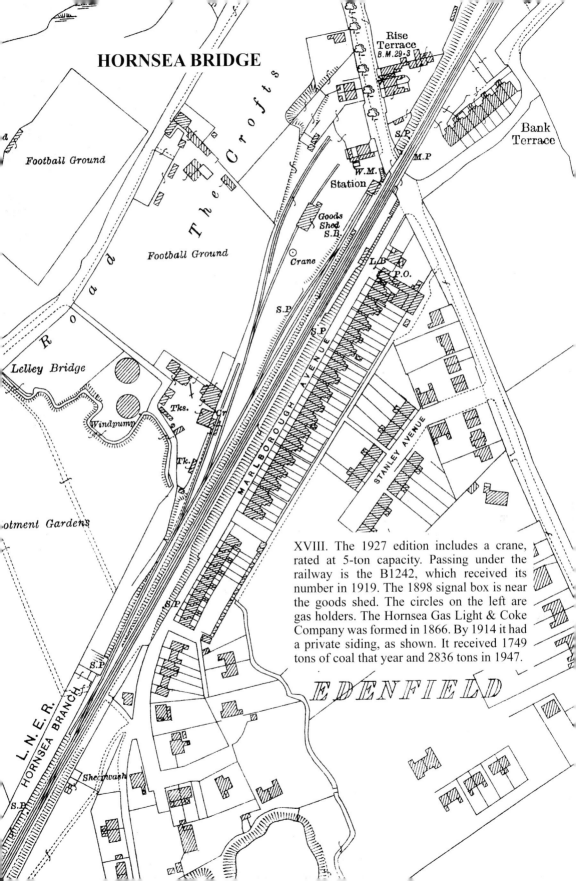

HORNSEA BRIDGE

XVIII. The 1927 edition includes a crane, rated at 5-ton capacity. Passing under the railway is the B1242, which received its number in 1919. The 1898 signal box is near the goods shed. The circles on the left are gas holders. The Hornsea Gas Light & Coke Company was formed in 1866. By 1914 it had a private siding, as shown. It received 1749 tons of coal that year and 2836 tons in 1947.

50.   This view north includes a train arriving from the terminus and details of the bridge. The steps descend between the gates, to reach the road. (P.Laming coll.)

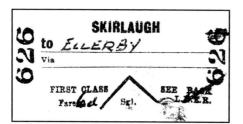

51.   This is the bridge after which the station is named and on it a down train waits to depart to the terminus. In deep shadow are the steps, which feature a bend. The handrails of the upside steps are near the right passenger beyond the bridge, in this view from the 1920s. (LOSA)

52.   This DMU driver's cab panorama is from 31st August 1956, as the train leaves for the terminus. Staffing ceased here on 4th January 1960 and the platforms were closed on 19th October 1964. The site has been built across. (R.M.Casserley)

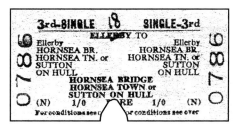

53.   A slightly later shot shows the incline up to the bridge from the north and the facilities for gentlemen nearest to us. The gas lamp had a convenient position for two purposes. (Colour-Rail.com)

54.   It is now clear that the goods yard was at a lower level. The embankment length can be seen on the map. Shunting is class 4MT 2-6-0 no. 43069, one of 162 introduced from 1947 and mostly used on the London Midland Region of BR. The yard was in use until 3rd May 1965. The tower is shown on the map as a windpump. (Colour-Rail.com)

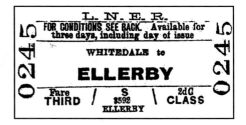

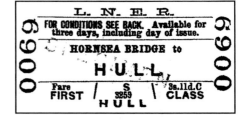

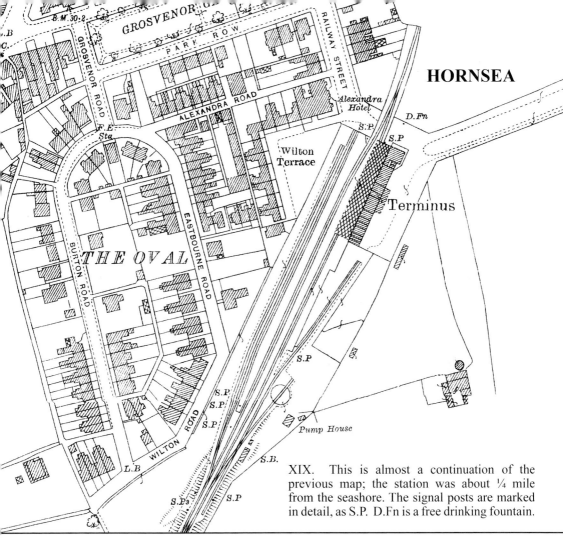

HORNSEA

XIX. This is almost a continuation of the previous map; the station was about ¼ mile from the seashore. The signal posts are marked in detail, as S.P. D.Fn is a free drinking fountain.

55. Diverse traffic was to be seen in around 1905 in what the card maker termed 'Seaside Station', but not one ankle was evident. The census recorded 2381 in 1901 and 5980 in 1961.(J.Alsop coll.)

56.   Standing at platform 2 on 2nd August 1949 is a 4-6-2T and compartment stock. The former is about to creep on to the headshunt to reverse. The gates were hand worked. (SLS coll.)

57.   Seen on the same day is 4-6-2T class A6 no. 69795. It had been built as a class W 4-6-0T. Another train had arrived from Hull at platform 3. No. 1 did not have an engine release line. (SLS coll.)

HORNSEA TOWN

58. The suffix TOWN was added on 25th September 1950. The locomotive water tank is on the left and the wheel for the water pump is turning fast to lift supplies from the well. Beyond the fine floral display is the 1888 signal box, which lasted until the end. (H.C.Casserley)

59. It is now 13th October 1956 and heading a train for Hull Paragon is class A8 4-6-2T no. 69860. The shed code on the smoke box is 53B, which was Hull Botanic Gardens. (N.D.Mundy)

60. A 1960 record features a packed DMU, with a family searching for a seat. Others look on, while we search for the Lion & Monocycle logo. The term was invented by your scribe. (R.Humm coll.)

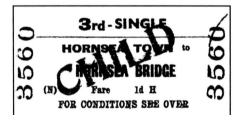

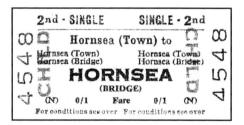

Table 21																			

HULL and HORNSEA (Second class only)

Miles		Week Days													Sundays (Commences 21st May)				
		a.m	a.m	a.m	p.m	p.m	pm S	pm	p.m	p.m E	p.m S	p.m A	p.m	pm	p.m D	p.m F	a.m	a.m	p.m	p.m	p.m
	Hull.........dep	6 19	7 42	9 25	12 25	1255	1 25	1 55	4 25	5 25	5 55	6 35	8 25	9 55	10 5	1125	1 45	6 45	7 10
1	Botanic Gardens ‡	6 23	7 46	9 29	12 29	1259	1 29	1 59	4 29	..	5 59	6 39	8 32	9 59	10 9	1129	1 49	6 49	7 14
1½	Stepney ‡	6 26	7 49	9 32	12 32	2	1 32	2	4 32	..	6 2	6 42	8 35	10 2	10 12	1132	1 52	6 52	7 17
2¼	Wilmington ‡	6 29	7 52	9 35	12 36	5	1 35	2 5	4 35	5 30	6 6	6 45	8 38	10 5	10 16	1136	1 56	6 55	7 20
2¾	Sutton-on-Hull ‡	6 34	..	9 40	12 40	10	1 40	2 10	4 40	5 35	6 10	6 50	8 43	1019	1021	1141	2 1	7 0	7 25
7	Swine ‡	6 38	..	..	12 44	..	..	..	4 44	..	..	6 54	8 47	1014	1025	..	2 5	7 4	7 29
9½	Ellerby ‡	6 46	8 5	9 47	12 50	1 17	1 47	2 17	4 50	5 42	6 17	7 0	8 53	1020	1031	..	2 11	7 10	7 35
10½	Whitedale ‡	6 49	..	..	12 53	..	1 53	2 23	4 53	..	6 20	8	8 56	1023	1034	..	2 14	7 13	7 38
12½	Sigglesthorne ‡	6 53	8 11	9 53	12 56	..	1 53	2 23	4 57	..	6 24	7	9 0	1027	1038	..	2 18	7 17	7 42
15	Hornsea Bridge........	6 57	8 15	9 57	1 0	1 25	1 57	2 27	5 1	5 50	6 28	7 11	9 4	1931	1042	..	2 22	7 21	7 46
15¾	Hornsea (Town) ... arr	6 59	8 17	9 59	1 2	1 27	1 59	2 29	5 3	5 52	6 30	7 18	9 6	1033	1044	1156	2 24	7 23	7 48

Miles		Week Days														Sundays (Commences 21st May)			
		a.m	a.m	a.m A	a.m	p.m	pm S	pm E	p.m S	p.m	p.m	p.m E	p.m D	p.m F	a.m	p.m	p.m	p.m	p.m
	Hornsea (Town)..... dep	7 5	7 50	8 30	1015	1 15	1 50	2 15	2 40	5 15	6 15	7 20	9 15	1045	1053	5 5	6 10	8 15
¾	Hornsea Bridge........	7 8	7 53	8 33	1018	1 18	1 53	2 18	2 43	5 18	6 18	7 23	9 18	1048	1056	5 8	..	8 18
3½	Sigglesthorne ‡	..	7 07	8 37	1022	..	2 22	..	2 47	5 22	6 22	7 27	9 22	1052	..	5 12	..	8 22
4½	Whitedale ‡	..	8 3	..	..	1 26	2 1	..	..	..	6 26	..	..	1056	11 4	5 16	..	8 26
5½	Ellerby ‡	7 17	8 4	8 43	1029	1 29	2 4	2 28	2 54	5 28	6 29	7 34	..	1059	11 7	5 19	..	8 29
8¼	Swine ‡	8 8	8 10	..	1034	1 35	2 10	..	..	..	6 35	..	..	11 5	1113	5 25	..	8 35
11	Sutton-on-Hull ‡.......	7 25	8 14	8 51	1038	1 39	2 14	2 36	3 4	5 36	6 39	..	..	11 9	1117	5 29	6 27	8 39
13	Wilmington ‡........	7 30	8 19	8 56	1043	1 44	2 19	..	3 9	5 41	6 44	7 45	..	1114	1122	5 34	6 32	8 44
13½	Stepney ‡............	7 33	8 22	8 59	1046	1 47	2 22	2 43	3 12	5 44	6 47	7 48	9 39	1117	1125	5 37	6 35	8 47
14	Botanic Gardens ‡.....	7 36	8 25	..	1049	1 50	2 25	2 46	3 15	5 47	6 50	7 50	9 42	1120	1128	5 40	6 38	8 50
15¾	Hull .... arr	7 40	8 29	9 7	1053	1 54	2 30	2 50	3 19	5 51	6 54	7 55	9 46	1125	1132	5 44	6 42	8 54

A Limited First class accommodation available   **D** Commences 22nd May   **E** or £ Except Saturdays   **F** Wednesdays and Saturdays
commences 24th May   **S** or $ Saturdays only   ‡ No staff in attendance

June 1961

61. The arches were similar to those at Whitby. We can enjoy a large Morris and a classic Armstrong Siddeley Sapphire, a rare vehicle enjoyed by your author in 1961. (R.Humm coll.)

62. The extent of the platforms and the seats provided for the crowds of the holiday visitors is impressive. Seen on 22nd July 1961, the flowers would soon be tall, but the nearest lamp is beyond the treatment. Blame the weather. (E.Wilmshurst)

63. Mourners are present on 17th October 1964, as total closure took place two days later. Staff remained at both stations to the end. It is evident on the right that gentlemen always had full roofing here. Ventilators are vertical below the top roof. (Colour-Rail.com)

64. Here is the sad situation on 24th May 1975, prior to work on flats, now known as apartments. Hornsea Bridge Goods Junction Box opened in 1898, with 24 levers. Hornsea Box opened in 1898, also, and was reframed with 30 levers in December 1929. (N.D.Mundy)

2. Hull to Withernsea

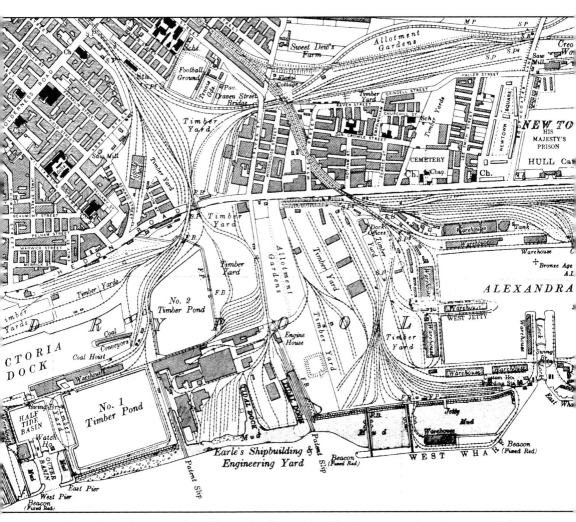

XX. The 1946 edition is at about 5ins to 1 mile and has Southcoates station shown as 'Sta', top left. The right part continues overleaf. Victoria station (also known as Victoria Dock station) was opened by the York & North Midland Railway on 1st June 1853 and was closed to passengers on 1st June 1864. It was named after Queen Victoria. The station remained in use as Drypool Goods Depot. Victoria Dock had a 40-ton capacity crane and is on the left. A new 25-lever signal box in 1903 lasted only until 1919. It was known as Joint Dock Junction.

Bradshaw, December 1895

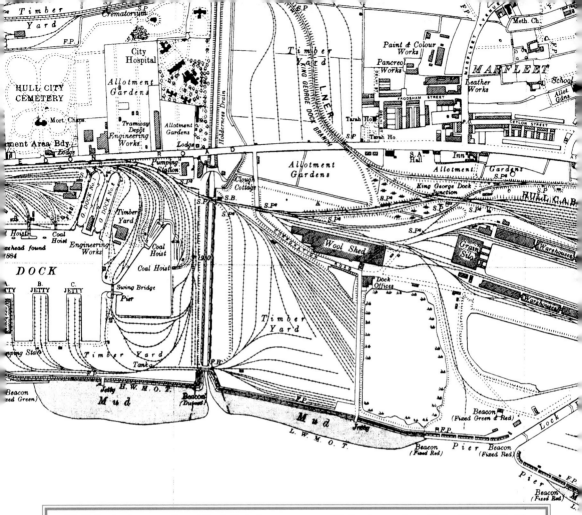

Hull to Antwerp—One of Gee & Co.'s Steamers—every Wednesday evening.—Fares, 21s. and 12s. 6d. The Hull Steam Packet Co.'s vessels (carrying post-office letter bags), every Saturday, at 6 p.m. Also an additional Steamer some other day of the week.—Fares, 21s. and 12s. 6d.

Hull to Aberdeen—A fast-sailing Clipper Schooner every Wednesday.

Hull to Barton—Week days, at 7 a.m., 12 noon, and 4 p.m. On Sundays, at 8½ a.m.; and 3 p.m.

Hull to Bremen—One of the Hull Steam Packet Co.'s Steamers, once a fortnight when the navigation is open

Hull to Brigg—Daily, at about 3 p.m., except Sundays.

Hull to Edinburgh (Leith)—The Brilliant—Average passage, 21 hours—March 6th, 1 p.m.; 13th, 5 p.m.; 20th, 1 p.m.; 27th, 5 p.m.—Fares, 14s. 6d. and 7s. 6d.; there and back, returning within a fortnight, 20s. and 10s.

Hull to Gainsborough—The Gainsborough Steam Packet Co.'s Vessels, Harlequin, or Columbine—Daily (Sunday excepted), 2½ hours before high water. The Hull Steam Packet Co.'s Vessels, daily.

Hull to Goole—One the of Hull Steam Packet Co.'s steamers, daily.

Hull to Grimsby—Daily, at high water.

Hull to Hamburgh—The Hull Steam Packet Co.'s vessels (carrying Her Majesty's Royal Mails), as opportunity offers. Fares, £2 and £1. Gee and Co's steamers as soon after 6 p.m. as possible. Sanderson and Co's Steamers will sail every Tuesday evening as soon after 6 p.m. as the tide permits. Fares £2 and £1.

Hull to Ipswich—The Cambridge, generally every Wednesday morning.

Hull to London—The General Steam Navigation Company's Steamers Waterwitch, or Vivid—every Tuesday and Saturday, at 1 p.m.—Fares, 17s. 6d. and 10s. The Hull Steam Packet Company's Steamers—every Monday, Wednesday, and Friday, at noon. Fares very low.

Hull to Lynn—The Lord Nelson, from Black Friargate Staithway—Average passage, 10 hours—March 4th, 11 p.m.; 8th, 1 a.m.; 12th, 4 a.m.; 14th, 7 p.m.; 18th, 9 p.m.; 21st, 12 night; 26th, 4 a.m.; 28th, 7 p.m. Fares, 7s. 6d. and 4s.

Hull to Newcastle—The Neptune, calling off Scarborough and Whitby—Every Wednesday at 7 a.m. Fares 5s. and 2s. The Atlas, from Black Friargate Staith—every Friday, as the tide permits. Fares, 4s. and 2s.

Hull to New Holland—Week days, 6, 6 30, 8½, 9, 10½ and 11½ a.m.; 1, 1½, 2½, 3 25, 4½, 5½, 6, and 7 13 p.m. Sundays—6½, 7½ and 8¼ a.m.; 12¼, 3, 5½, and 7 13 p.m.

Hull to Rotterdam—The Sea Gull or Emerald Isle—Average passage, 22 hours—every Wednesday and Saturday, as soon after 3½ p.m. as the tide permits.

Hull to Wisbeach—The Forager, from the Humber Dock—Average passage, 12 hours—Every Friday afternoon. Fares, 7s. 6d. and 4s.

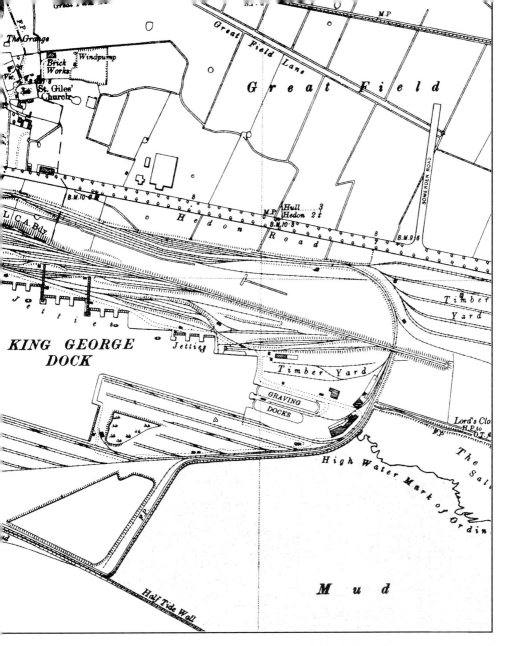

XXI. This map continues from the last one. Much of the dock equipment was operated by electricity, supplied at 440V by the Hull Corporation, including conveyors, cranes and dock lighting, as well as powering pumps used to supply hydraulic power. King George V opened the right Dock on 26th June 1914 and in 1919 a massive grain silo was completed. It was demolished in 2010-11. The double track (top left) is shown again on map XXIII of Marfleet. Left of centre on the left page is Holderness Drain signal box, which opened on 17th January 1921. It had 30 levers and closed on 25th February 1968.

← Hull sailings (UK and Europe), *Bradshaw's General Monthly Railway and Steam Navigation Guide*, March 1850.

SOUTHCOATES

65. This view south shows the island platform, which was in use from 1st June 1864 to 19th October 1964. Freight traffic ceased officially on 3rd March 1969. There had been a footbridge for access, from the east side. There is now no trace of the station. (Stations UK)

66. The signal box was north of the platform, on Holderness Road, and is seen in 1963. The bay window would be good for traffic observations, but not pedestrians under it. The 1904 box had 70 levers and two gate wheels. Trams crossed here until 17th February 1940 and the frame had only 41 levers from 1944. Closure came on 14th December 1968. (R.Humm coll.)

SOUTH OF SOUTHCOATES

Victoria Dock

67.   Shunting in 1954 is class Y1 Sentinel no. 68148, which had single-speed gearing. There had been 24 in this class. During the Hull Blitz, the site was hit by bombs three times, with the yard's stables set alight on one occasion. Freight traffic continued to 1968. (N.Stead/Transport Treasury)

King George Dock

XXII. The 2006 diagram has this dock lower left, with the Quay numbers shown, and the Queen Elizabeth extension below it. It was opened in 1969. By 2010, there were passenger services to Zeebrugge and roll on-roll off ferries using the docks. A vegetable oil refinery was opened in 1984.

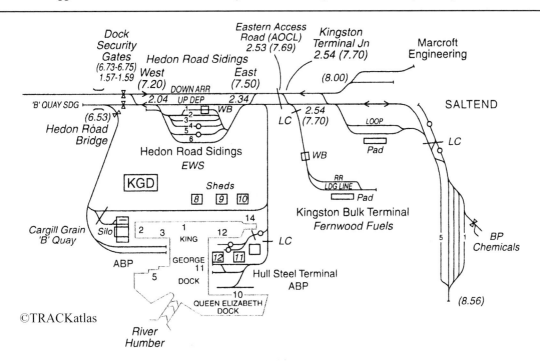

©TRACKatlas

68.   The security gates are top left on the diagram. Arriving with empty hoppers for loading with imported coal for Drax Power Station on 1st August 2005 is no. 66545. Another major import for it was biomass from Scandinavia, from 2013. (P.D.Shannon)

69.   The impressive train is seen an hour or so later, together with the long conveyor belt in the background. It took 40 minutes to load an entire train, using seven mechanical shovels. The first such trains were run in September 1991. There were seven on the day witnessed. (P.D.Shannon)

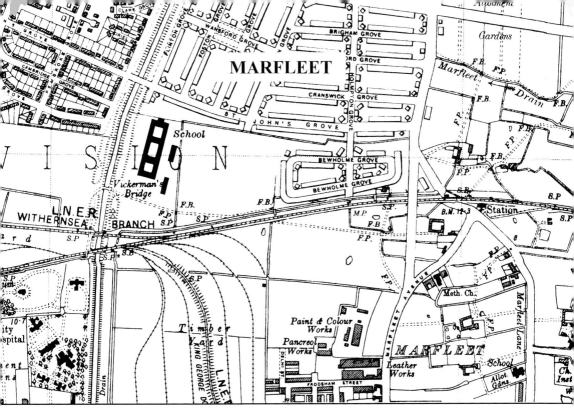

XXIII. The station is on the right of this 1946 extract, which is scaled at 6ins to 1 mile. The branch to the lower border continues on the left page of map XXI.

70.   A 1962 panorama looking east includes a van in use as a parcels shed. The goods yard was beyond the right fence and closed on 1st May 1972, passenger service having ceased on 19th October 1964. The track eastwards to Hedon was not used after 1968. The building on the right became a home. The 25-lever signal box served from December 1903 until December 1968. (Stations UK)

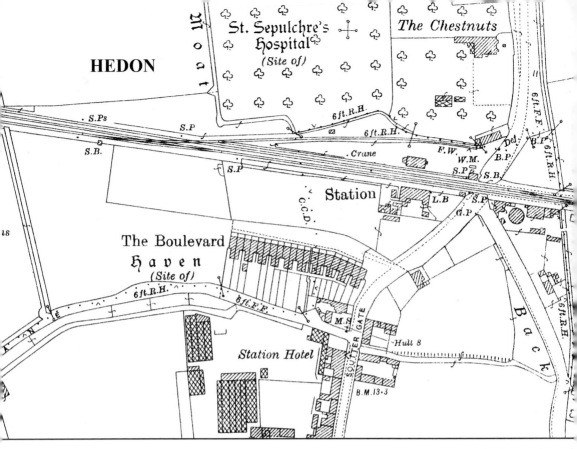

XXIV. The 1927 map includes the northern part of the village. There is a 5-ton crane in the goods yard and a headshunt is the top line at the left border. As only one platform was provided, two signal boxes are shown, to allow all trains to use it. Hedon Gas Works (right) took about 660 tons of coal per annum. It was purchased by the East Hull Gas Company in about 1930 and would have ceased production soon after.

71.   The two signals on the right are for trains to Withernsea. The two on the left have short arms and are for shunting movements. The local population was 1010 in 1901 and 2410 in 1961. The box was used in 1903-66. It had 29 levers and a gate wheel. (J.Alsop coll.)

72.   A train runs in from Hull. It will have just passed through Hedon Racecourse station, which was only open on race days, between 28th August 1888 and 1909, when horse racing was terminated. The station was briefly re-opened as Hedon Halt between 14th August 1948 and 23rd October 1948, to serve speedway meetings. (P.Laming coll.)

73.   On the platform is a child in an early large-wheeled perambulator. Between the two groups of wagons is a boarded crossing, which aided the movement of parcels between the goods shed and a van on the loop. On the left are coal wagons with bottom doors, standing above the coal drops into which they discharged. (R.Humm coll.)

74. This view west is shortly before closure to passengers on 19th October 1964. Freight service ended here on 3rd June 1968, but the route west hereof closed completely in 1965. The house became a dwelling and printing was undertaken in the goods shed. (Stations UK)

XXV. The 1920 edition at 2ins to 1 mile includes the single line on the right. It ran east for two miles from the level crossing on the right, known as Magdalen Gates. It was ¼ mile longer on the 1911 edition and continued to the next station, Rye Hill. At the top border is part of the village of Preston. There was a station called Preston West End Gate during part of 1854, near 'The Limes' level crossing. The sidings on the left are on the right of map XXII, but one of these extends to a salt works, which opened in 1914.

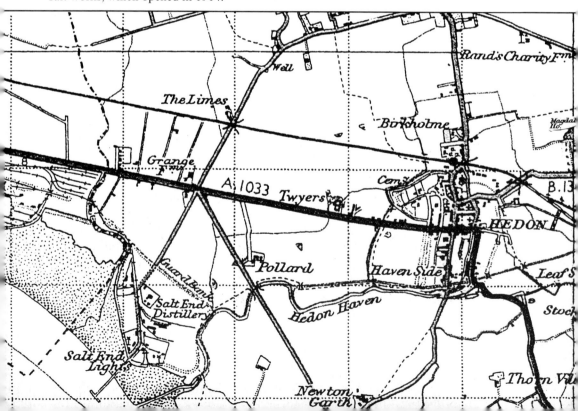

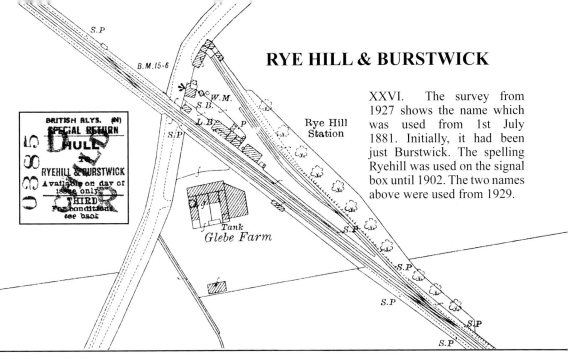

RYE HILL & BURSTWICK

XXVI. The survey from 1927 shows the name which was used from 1st July 1881. Initially, it had been just Burstwick. The spelling Ryehill was used on the signal box until 1902. The two names above were used from 1929.

February 1884

* Station for Easington.]	HULL and WITHERNSEA.—North Eastern.																[Sndys.		
Fares.	Paragon Sta.,	mrn	mrn	mrn	aft	aft	aft	**Sndys**		Up.	mrn	mrn	mrn	aft	aft	aft	aft	mrn	aft
1 cl.|2 cl.|3 cl.										Withernsea	7 55	8 45	11 5	3 20	6 25	7 25	9 50	9 20	5 25
0 3|0 2|0 1	Hull ....dep	6 38	7 5	9 50	2 0	4 51	5 40	8 40	8 0	Patrington*	8 3	8 52	11 13	3 28	6 32	7 33	9 57	9 28	5 33
0 4|0 3|0 1½	BotnicGrdns	6 42		9 54	2 4	4 55		8 44	8 4	Winestead ..	8 6		11 16	3 31		7 36	Sig.	9 31	5 36
0 4|0 3|0 2	Stepney	6 45	7 10	9 57	2 7	4 58		8 47	8 7	Ottringham ..	8 12	8 58	11 22	3 37	6 38	7 42	10 5	9 37	5 42
0 6|0 4|0 3	Sculcoates ..	6 48		10 0	2 10	5 1		8 50	8 10	Keyingham ..	8 17	9 2	11 27	3 42	6 42	7 47	10 10	9 42	5 47
0 8|0 6|0 5	Southcoates .	6 52	7 15	10 4	2 14	5 5	5 48	8 54	8 14	4 20	Rye Hill	8 22		11 32	3 47	Sat.	7 52	10 15	9 47	5 52
2 0|0 16|0 8	Hedon	6 57		10 9	2 19	5 10		8 59	8 19	4 25	Hedon	8 28	9 9	11 38	3 53	6 50	7 58	10 21	9 53	5 58
1 4|1 1|0 10½	Rye Hill	7 10		10 22	2 32	5 23		9 12	8 32	4 38	Marfleet ...	8 35		11 45	4 0	....	8 5	10 28	10 0	6 5
1 8|1 4|1 0	Keyingham ..	7 15	7 32	10 27	2 37	5 28	6 3	9 17	8 37	4 43	Southcoates .	8 40	9 18	11 50	4 5	7 0	8 10	10 33	10 5	6 10
2 0|1 6|1 0	Ottringham .	7 20	7 36	10 32	2 42	5 33	6 7	9 22	8 42	4 48	Sculcoates ..	8 44		11 54	4 9	....	8 14			6 14
2 2|1 6|1 0	Winestead ..	7 26		10 38	2 48	5 39		9 28	8 48	4 54	Stepney	8 47		11 57	4 12	7 6	8 17	10 39		6 17
2 0|1 6|1 0	Patrington* .	7 29		10 41	2 51	5 42	6 14	9 31	8 51	4 57	BotnicGrdns	8 50		12 0	4 15	7 9	8 20	10 42		6 20
2 0|1 6|1 0	Withernsea .	7 39	7 50	10 51	3 1	5 52	6 23	9 41	9 1	5 7	Hull 260 arr	8 58	9 31	12 8	4 23	7 17	8 28	10 50		6 28

75. The team pose in about 1900, with three watch chains and one daughter enhancing the record. The name shown was in use until 23rd September 1929. (P.Laming coll.)

76. Sadly, details were not recorded, but the good news is that the building survived and was extended. It served Station House Tool Hire. The signal box lasted from 1902 until 1964. It had 27 levers. About a mile to the east was the 20-lever Kelsey Hill box, from 1904 to 1927. It served a large gravel pit, which had been used during the construction of the line. It can be found on map XXIX. The engine appears to be an ex-GNR class C12. (P.Laming coll.)

77. The full and final name is seen from a passing train on 31st August 1956. Closure came on 19th October 1964, but goods items were accepted up to 3rd May 1965. The level crossing is in the distance. (H.C.Casserley)

78. A panorama from the level crossing includes the goods shed, water buckets for unwanted fires, bowls for floral joys and pleasure for chimney pot students. (Stations UK)

June 1961

Table 22																						
HULL and WITHERNSEA (Second class only)																						
	Week Days																**Sundays** (Commences 21st May)					
Miles	a.m	a.m		p.m	p.m		p.m	p.m		p.m	p.m		p.m	p.m		p.m		a.m	a.m		p.m	pm	p.m
				S							**E**					**H**	**D**						
	Hull .... der	6 50	9 40	..	12 8	1240	..	1 40	3 35	..	4 40	5 5	..	5 35	6 10	..	6 40	8 35	..	9 40	..	9 55	..	1035	..	1 35	..	6 25	..	7 5
1 Botanic Gardens ‡	6 54	9 44	..	1212	1244	..	1 44	3 39	..	4 44	..	..	..	6 14	..	6 44	8 39	..	9 44	..	9 59	..	1039	..	1 39	..	6 29	..	7 9
1½ Stepney ‡	6 57	9 47	..	1215	1247	..	1 47	3 42	..	4 47	..	..	..	6 17	..	6 47	8 42	..	9 47	..	10 2	..	1042	..	1 42	..	6 32	..	7 12
2½ Wilmington ‡	7 0	9 50	..	1218	1251	..	1 51	3 45	..	4 51	5 10	..	5 40	6 20	..	6 50	8 45	..	9 50	..	10 6	..	1045	..	1 46	..	6 35	..	7 15
3½ Southcoates ‡	7 3	9 53	..	1221	1254	..	1 54	3 48	..	4 54	5 13	..	5 43	6 23	..	6 53	8 48	..	9 53	..	10 9	..	1049	..	1 49	..	6 38	..	7 18
6½ Marfleet ‡	7 8	9 58	..	1225	1259	..	1 59	3 53	..	4 69	5 18	..	5 47	6 28	..	6 58	8 53	..	9 57	..	1014	..	1054	..	1 54	..	6 43	..	7 23
5½ Hedon ‡ [Burstwick	7 12	11 3	..	1230	1 4	..	2 4	3 58	..	5 4	5 23	..	5 52	6 33	..	7 3	8 58	..	10 2	..	1019	..	..	..	1 59	..	6 48	..	7 28
10½ Rye Hill and ‡	7 18	11 8	..	1235	1 9	..	2 9	4 3	..	5 9	..	..	5 57	6 39	..	7 8	9 3	..	10 7	..	1024	..	..	..	2 4	..	6 53	..	7 32
12½ Keyingham ‡	7 22	1112	..	1239	1 13	..	2 13	4 7	..	5 13	..	..	6 1	6 43	..	7 12	9 7	..	1011	..	1028	..	..	..	2 8	..	6 57	..	7 37
14 Ottringham ‡	7 26	1116	..	1243	1 17	..	2 17	4 11	..	5 17	..	..	6 5	6 47	..	7 16	9 11	..	1015	..	1032	..	..	..	2 12	..	7 1	..	7 41
17 Patrington ‡	7 33	1123	..	1249	1 24	..	2 24	4 18	..	5 24	..	..	6 11	6 54	..	7 22	9 17	..	1021	..	1039	..	..	..	2 19	..	7 8	..	7 49
20½ Withernsea .... arr	7 39	1129	..	1255	1 30	..	2 30	4 24	..	5 30	5 45	..	6 17	7 0	..	7 28	9 23	..	1027	..	1045	..	1119	..	2 25	..	7 14	..	7 54

	Week Days																**Sundays** (Commences 21st May)					
Miles	a.m	a.m		a.m	a.m		a.m	pm		p.m	p.m		p.m	p.m		p.m		am	p.m		p.m	pm	pm
					S											**H**	**D**						
	Withernsea .... der	6 20	6 45	..	7 50	8 15	..	1040	1 0	..	1 37	2 40	..	4 35	5 40	..	7 40	9 35	..	1045	..	1053	4 35	..	6 10	7 5	..	8 20	..
3½ Patrington ‡	..	6 51	..	7 56	..	..	1046	..	..	1 43	2 46	..	4 41	5 46	..	7 46	..	..	1051	..	1059	..	..	..	..	..	8 26	..
6½ Ottringham ‡	6 31	6 57	..	8 2	8 26	..	1152	..	..	1 49	2 52	..	4 47	5 52	..	7 52	9 46	..	1057	..	11 5	..	..	..	..	..	8 32	..
8½ Keyingham ‡	6 34	7 0	..	8 5	..	..	1055	..	..	1 52	..	..	4 50	5 55	..	..	9 49	..	11 0	..	11 8	..	..	..	..	..	8 35	..
10 Rye Hill and ‡	6 38	7 4	..	8 9	8 32	..	1059	..	..	1 56	2 58	..	4 54	6 0	..	7 58	9 53	..	11 4	..	1112	..	..	..	..	..	8 39	..
12½ Hedon ‡ [Burstwick	6 42	7 8	..	8 13	8 36	..	11 3	..	..	2 0	3 2	..	4 58	6 4	..	8 2	9 57	..	11 8	..	1116	..	6 30	..	..	..	8 43	..
15½ Marfleet ‡	6 47	7 13	..	8 18	8 41	..	11 9	..	..	2 6	3 8	..	5 6	6 10	..	..	..	..	1113	..	1122	5 0	..	6 36	7 30	..	8 48	..
17 Southcoates ‡	6 51	7 17	..	8 22	8 45	..	1113	..	..	2 10	3 12	..	5 9	6 14	..	8 9	10 4	..	1117	..	1126	5 4	..	6 40	7 34	..	8 52	..
18½ Wilmington ‡	6 54	7 20	..	8 25	8 48	..	1116	..	..	2 13	..	..	5 12	6 17	..	8 12	..	..	1120	..	1129	5 7	..	6 43	7 37	..	8 55	..
19 Stepney ‡	6 57	7 23	..	8 28	..	..	1119	..	..	2 16	3 18	..	5 15	6 20	..	8 15	1010	..	1124	..	1132	5 10	..	6 46	7 40	..	8 58	..
19½ Botanic Gardens ‡..	7 0	7 26	..	8 31	..	..	1123	..	..	2 20	3 21	..	5 18	6 23	..	8 19	1014	..	1128	..	1135	5 14	..	6 50	7 44	..	9 2	..
20½ Hull .... arr	7 5	7 30	..	8 35	8 54	..	1127	1 33	..	2 24	3 25	..	5 22	6 27	..	8 23	1018	..	1132	..	1139	5 18	..	6 54	7 48	..	9 6	..

D Tuesdays and Saturdays only. Commences 23rd May   **E** Except Saturdays   **H** Commences 22nd May   **S** Saturdays only
‡ No staff in attendance

KEYINGHAM

79. The 1901 census recorded just 549 souls. The crossing for passengers is close to the gates and under the watchful eyes of the signalman. The box was in use in 1904-64. (P.Laming coll.)

80. A 1962 photo reveals a tidy site, although staffing had ceased on 4th January 1960. Closure to passengers came on 19th October 1964 and the building became a dwelling, with a car repair business on the approach road. (Stations UK)

XXVII. The 1927 issue reveals that this station is unlike the others in that it has sidings on both sides of the road. The weighing machine is unusually distant from the main building.

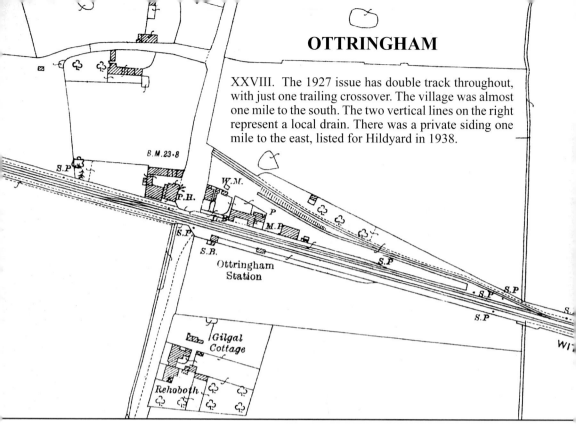

OTTRINGHAM

XXVIII. The 1927 issue has double track throughout, with just one trailing crossover. The village was almost one mile to the south. The two vertical lines on the right represent a local drain. There was a private siding one mile to the east, listed for Hildyard in 1938.

Ottringham
Station

Gilgal
Cottage

Rehoboth

81. We now look west and see all the buildings, except the goods shed. We can look through the 21-lever signal box on the left; it was operational from 1890 to 1964. Both closure dates are as in caption 80. (P.Laming coll.)

82. The box and waiting shelter are clearer in this photograph from a train from Hull on 31st August 1956. A very secret and high-powered radio transmitter station was created nearby by the BBC during WWII. It sent out its Home Service to Northern Lincolnshire and Southern Yorkshire, plus propaganda to Germany and beyond. There was no TV. (H.C.Casserley)

83. This panorama in the other direction is from 1962 and includes boards in the foreground over a drainage pit. The BBC had occupied 95 acres and went on to use the massive mast for the Light Programme, until closure in 1953. The house avoided destruction. (Stations UK)

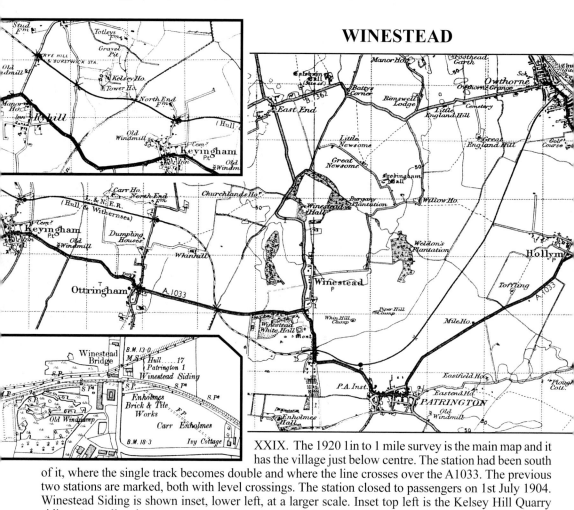

WINESTEAD

XXIX. The 1920 1in to 1 mile survey is the main map and it has the village just below centre. The station had been south of it, where the single track becomes double and where the line crosses over the A1033. The previous two stations are marked, both with level crossings. The station closed to passengers on 1st July 1904. Winestead Siding is shown inset, lower left, at a larger scale. Inset top left is the Kelsey Hill Quarry siding. An earlier closure was on 1st September 1870 for Hollym Gate, which is near the right border. However, goods traffic continued until 9th January 1953, under the name of 'Hollym Gate Siding'.

84. Goods traffic continued until 1st May 1956 and the remains were photographed on 26th May 1975. The location was named 'Winestead Siding' from 1904 until closure. We are looking towards Hull. The 36-lever signal box had a gate wheel and opened in 1904. (N.D.Mundy)

PATRINGTON

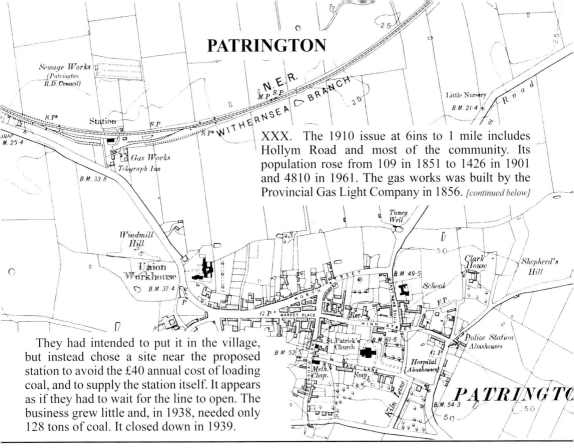

XXX. The 1910 issue at 6ins to 1 mile includes Hollym Road and most of the community. Its population rose from 109 in 1851 to 1426 in 1901 and 4810 in 1961. The gas works was built by the Provincial Gas Light Company in 1856. *[continued below]*

They had intended to put it in the village, but instead chose a site near the proposed station to avoid the £40 annual cost of loading coal, and to supply the station itself. It appears as if they had to wait for the line to open. The business grew little and, in 1938, needed only 128 tons of coal. It closed down in 1939.

85. A 1905 postcard features a wide range of staff and families, plus two ornate columns. All wooden cartwheels had iron tyres. Most advertisements related to Hull. (LOSA)

86. A greater authority appeared on a later card, with one top hat and one bowler evident. Barrow wheels were more reliable, being cast iron and steel was often used elsewhere in the construction.
(R.Humm coll.)

87. The goods yard and its dock are evident, and the jib of the 3-ton crane appears above the group of wagons. The signal box was completed in about 1904, but was destroyed in a shunting accident in 1942. The first box had 35 levers and the second one had 22. (J.Alsop coll.)

88. The 1962 panorama includes the replacement box, with a contemporary flat roof. It was worked until station closure in 1964. The crane and loading gauge are in the distance. Goods traffic ceased on 3rd May 1965. (Stations UK)

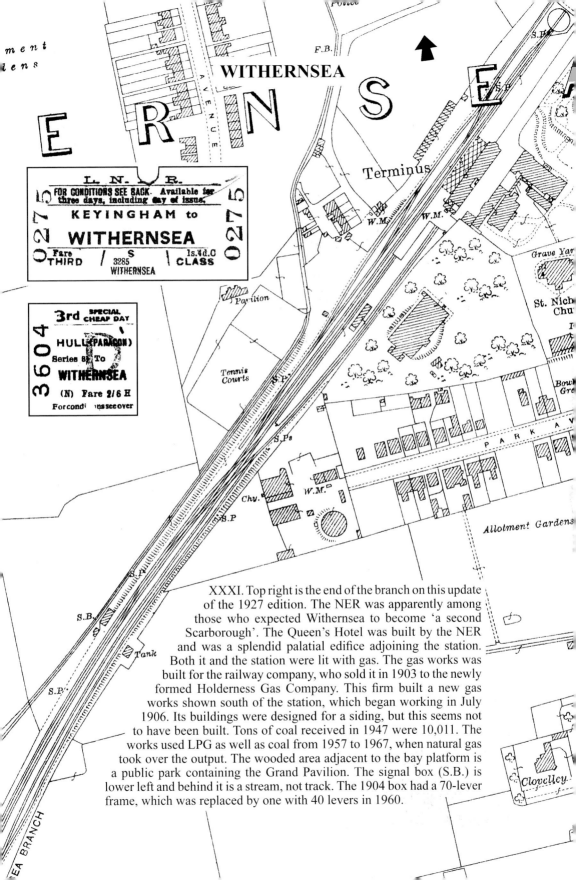

WITHERNSEA

XXXI. Top right is the end of the branch on this update of the 1927 edition. The NER was apparently among those who expected Withernsea to become 'a second Scarborough'. The Queen's Hotel was built by the NER and was a splendid palatial edifice adjoining the station. Both it and the station were lit with gas. The gas works was built for the railway company, who sold it in 1903 to the newly formed Holderness Gas Company. This firm built a new gas works shown south of the station, which began working in July 1906. Its buildings were designed for a siding, but this seems not to have been built. Tons of coal received in 1947 were 10,011. The works used LPG as well as coal from 1957 to 1967, when natural gas took over the output. The wooded area adjacent to the bay platform is a public park containing the Grand Pavilion. The signal box (S.B.) is lower left and behind it is a stream, not track. The 1904 box had a 70-lever frame, which was replaced by one with 40 levers in 1960.

89. The main platform is seen in about 1901, with a coach in the bay platform. The massive hotel building on the right was converted to a convalescent home, as insufficient holiday visitors appeared. (J.Alsop coll.)

90. A view from the coast end of the line reveals the generous weather protection needed. The end of a coach is in the bay platform, while four coaches stand on the loop. (R.Humm coll.)

91. Endless advertisements ruin the view of a 2-4-0 on the turntable. It had just arrived with the train standing above its dome. Crowds are emerging from it, while a goods train waits on the right. (LOSA)

92. For many decades, locomotives had been turned in this manner, although an 0-6-0 would be around 40 tons. The 'Kinema' had become a trendy term verbally in a number of districts. This undated view is pre-BR, as there is no smokebox number plate. The table was 46ft 6ins in length. The loco is an ex-NER class J21. (R.Humm coll.)

↑   93. The roof name has changed and the turntable pit has become clear. The population had grown from 109 in 1851 to 1426 in 1901 and 4810 in 1961. The second signal box opened in 1904 with 70 levers. They were reduced to 40 in September 1960. Closure came with the line. (LOSA)

➜   94. The extent of the toilet facilities is on the right. No. 2 refers to the bay platform. Heading the 4.20pm to Hull on 20th October 1954 is class L1 2-6-4T no. 67763. (R.Humm coll.)

↓   95. A panorama from 31st August 1956 features fine floral work, all of platform 2 and the LNER's choice for lavatory windows: a white oval glass. Passengers had to choose carefully, as there is not even a corridor in the nearest coach. (R.M.Casserley)

96.   Seen on the same day taking water is no. 67677, a 2-6-2T of class V1, later becoming 4MT. The water was pumped by wind power to a high tank. Passenger traffic ceased on 19th October 1964, but staffing remained until then. The site was adapted for an open-air market and was later used for a supermarket and car park. (H.C.Casserley)

97.   Ready to depart on 22nd July 1961 is a class 106 DMU, a type often fitted with Leyland engines. There were only two windows at each end of all these units. The goods yard had a 5-ton crane and closed on 3rd May 1965. (E.Wilmshurst)

3. Spurn Head Railway

Howard M. Frost

← XXXII. The 1947 issue at 1in to 1 mile shows a simplified and slightly shortened version of the line, presumably for security reasons. All indication of military occupation (which continued until 1956-59) is missed out. 'L.B.& C.G.Sta' refers to Life Boat and Coast Guard Stations.

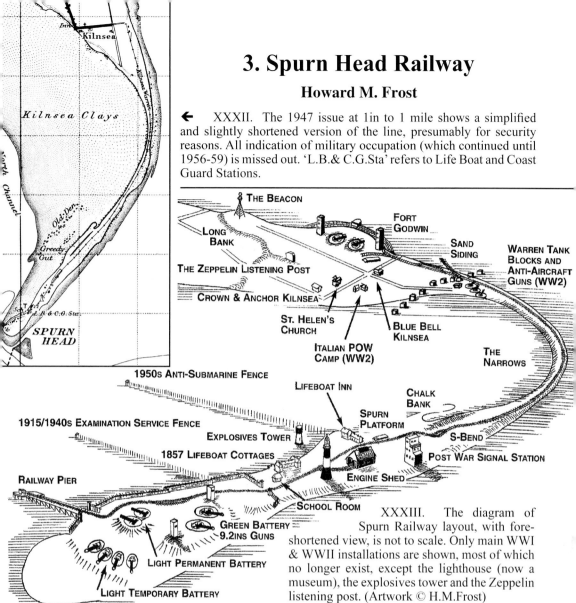

XXXIII. The diagram of Spurn Railway layout, with fore-shortened view, is not to scale. Only main WWI & WWII installations are shown, most of which no longer exist, except the lighthouse (now a museum), the explosives tower and the Zeppelin listening post. (Artwork © H.M.Frost)

This section is based on Howard Frost's booklet, *Sailing the Rails,* **published by the Spurn Heritage Coast in 2001 and on Ken Hartley's earlier work on the railway, published by the Industrial Railway Society in 1976.**

CONSTRUCTION

In the first half of the 20th Century, large construction projects often used portable standard or narrow gauge rail systems to move heavy materials around a large site. In the case of Spurn, the building of two military forts some four miles apart in such a wild, sandy and isolated area could hardly have been done in any other way at that time. Five different industrial saddle tank engines were used, although no close-up photos of these engines appear to have been taken at Spurn, except for *Kenyon*. Few people had cameras then and casual visitors were probably restricted. However, some of these locomotives might be spotted but not identified on the aerial photos which follow. Four left the site on completion of the project. The fifth engine, *Kenyon*, was bought by the Army and retained at Spurn until about 1930.

98. *Frances*, an 0-4-0 Hudswell Clarke saddle tank, was built in 1895. It worked on railway construction for the Lancashire, Derbyshire & East Coast Railway and after its stint at Spurn was used on London County Council housing projects amongst others. It is pictured at Becontree in Essex in 1931. (R.A.Wheeler/K.E.Hartley coll.)

99. *Somerton* was an 0-4-0 Hudswell Clarke built specially for C.J.Wills in 1903. It worked on the Grimsby and Immingham Docks projects before coming to Spurn. Later it was sold on to a Darlington Foundry. It was scrapped in Stockton around 1950. The photo shows it with a 'Paddy Train' on the GWR's North Warwickshire line. (F.Jones/K.E.Hartley coll.)

100. *Bombay* was a Manning Wardle 0-6-0 built in 1906, and named after its first contract in Bombay, India. It was later acquired by C.J.Wills. After Spurn, it worked in London and eventually ended up in Dagenham Docks, Essex, from 1938 to 1956, where this photo was taken in 1947. (G.Alliez/K.E.Hartley coll.)

101. *Lord Mayor*: This 0-4-0 Hudswell Clarke saddle tank was built in 1893 and acquired by C.J.Wills in 1903. After leaving Spurn it worked on sites in London, Leicestershire, Birmingham, Leeds and Liverpool. In the London area it worked on sites constructing some 27,000 homes at Becontree in Essex. It still exists as part of the Middleton Railway Trust's collection in Leeds. In more recent times it has also been on display at the Keighley & Worth Valley Railway. This atmospheric picture shows it at work in Cliff Hill Granite Quarries at Croft in Leicestershire. (K.E.Hartley coll.)

102. These photos, dated 16th August 1917, are part of a set covering much of the peninsula. No-one knows who took them but it seems likely they were requested by C.J.Wills and were probably taken from a balloon. They were presented to the Spurn Heritage Coast archive by someone who explained he had just rescued them from being burned on a bonfire by his father who was tidying up: 'Would they be of any interest?' he asked. A boat, partially hidden by smoke, is docked at the pier-head with a line of wagons along the pier, and a steam engine with more wagons just round the sharp bend. Visitors to the area today can still see remnants of this military occupation. The pier is gone, but its gateway in the sea wall is still just about visible.
(H.M.Frost coll./
Spurn Heritage Coast)

103. The right page shows Spurn Fort with buildings virtually complete. The two large circles are the emplacements for 9.2in guns, whilst other circles indicate smaller guns. At the top is the passing loop. An engine and wagons can be seen and possibly a steam crane as well. Look at the sandy tracks to deduce where the construction railway lines might have run and note the marks on the beach indicating one or more probable sand sidings. Beach sand was used for much of the construction.
(H.M.Frost coll./
Spurn Heritage Coast)

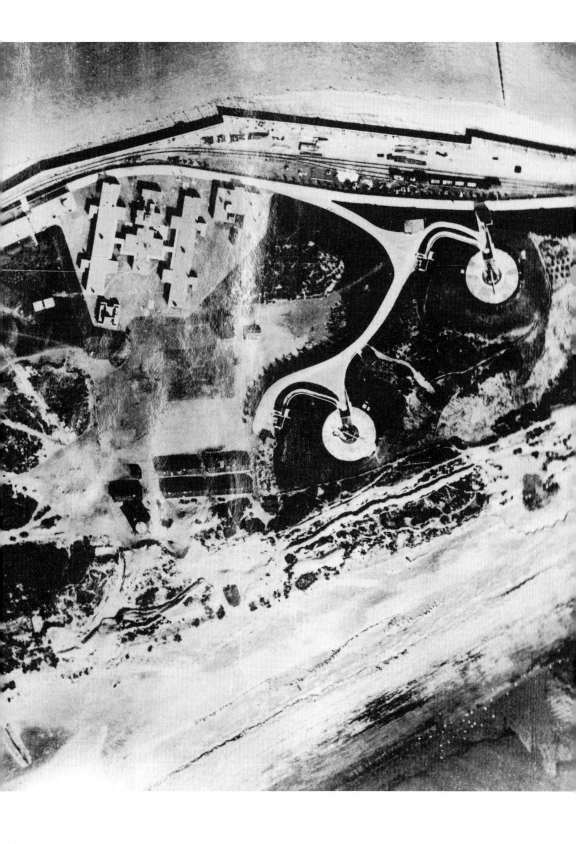

North Marsh Road

FORT GODWIN

Hospital

Barracks

KILNSEA

Gwendene Café

Blue Bell Inn

Kilnsea
Headland

9.2ins guns

Water siding

Officers' Mess

passing loop

Sand siding

Spun Head Railway

North
Sea

Kilnsea Warren

← 104. This Godwin Fort aerial view shows a complicated set of lines and turnouts plus one of two sand sidings (the other being further south). Various wagons and possibly two steam engines are visible plus what appears to be the North London coach, later retained by the Army. Follow the track upwards from the bottom and trace the left-hand curve to the edge where you can see the pale rectangular shape and ramp of the Blue Bell platform with its crane. The inset map (circa 1926) shows the simplified layout paid for by the Army. There were two other platforms at Godwin Fort, one inside the railings for loading armaments and one close to the Officer's Mess for passengers. (H.M.Frost coll./Spurn Heritage Coast)

105. This unidentified B-type Drewry railcar was probably photographed at the Spurn Point end of the line. It was identified as being present on one of the aerial photos, so probably arrived prior to 1918 and stayed on the line until being incorporated into the 'Bitsa' (see photo 112). Bessie Miles travelled on this vehicle in October 1920 and wrote in her diary: '*The Dury Car (sic) was a sort of glorified trolley driven by a motor… The driver sat nonchantly with his back to the direction in which we travelled [along] the 4 miles of sandy peninsula [where] we were indeed at the edge of beyond.*' The use of at least three different Drewry railcars at Spurn resulted in all the railcars, including the later Hardy and the Hudswell Clarke, being known to residents and visitors alike as 'The Drewry'.
(E.E.Landucci/H.M.Frost coll.)

106. The route of Bessie Miles journey 'to the edge of beyond': a view southward at Spurn's Narrow Neck. The print was abstracted from a 1920's lantern slide discovered at Scarborough's Woodend Museum. (I.Massey/Scarborough Borough Council)

BETWEEN THE WARS

107. *Kenyon* was an 0-6-0 Vulcan Foundry saddle tank built at Newton-le-Willows in 1888 and used for building the Manchester Ship Canal and Immingham Docks. It was bought second-hand by C.J.Wills for the Spurn contract and later sold on to the War Dept. for continued use at Spurn. It always faced south as there were no turning facilities on the line. Painted black with red buffer beams, it operated a regular one coach train for passengers (usually with a single open wagon attached) until 1929, after which it was scrapped on site by a Hull dealer. It was in poor condition and photos show it operating with first two then no coupled wheels at all. The coach, thought to be ex-North London stock, was a non-corridor type with five separate compartments, entered via separate doors. Although it became very tatty over the years, it not only lasted until the railway was closed in 1951/52, but the body still remains in use in a garden in Kilnsea!
(*Railway Magazine*/H.M.Frost coll.)

108. An Itala racing car, brought to Spurn by Lieutenant Lees, a Royal Engineer, around 1918/20, was converted to run on the rails and was said to have reached 60mph along the track on one occasion. After a crash crossing a turnout, which was not fully set, it was converted into 'the Bitsa' (see photo 112). On one occasion in this guise (1922) it was photographed for the *Eastern Morning News* sporting a sail and processing along the line with two other sail bogies.
(E.E.Landucci/ H.M.Frost coll.)

109. This is Baguley Cars Ltd No. 1119, as supplied to the WD at Spurn on 21st January 1920. It was a 12-seater delivered by rail to Patrington and brought by road to Spurn. For reasons unknown it left Spurn soon after delivery.
(Baguley-Drewry Ltd/ K.E.Hartley coll.)

110. The third and final Drewry car to work at Spurn was this 6-seater C-type railcar. It had two upholstered seats fitted with reversible backrests and could be driven from either end. It caught fire and was destroyed sometime before 1930.
(C.Leonard/H.M.Frost coll.)

111. Following the loss of the C-type Drewry and *Kenyon* around 1930, a new bigger railcar was bought from Hardy Motors Ltd of Slough. It had doors in the middle and could be driven from either end. The four wheels lacked any springing, giving a very hard ride. It was maintained by Kingston Engineering Co. in Hull, where it is seen, necessitating periodic long road journeys to and from Hull. (Kingston Engineering (Hull) Ltd/H.M.Frost coll.)

112. The lifeboatmen built and operated 'The Bitsa' - 'made of bits of this and bits of that'. In front, the working remains of the Itala is with an old cistern as radiator. The seats came from the B-Type Drewry, the frame of which had been converted into a tank carrying wagon to bring drinking water to Spurn Point. The photo was taken in front of the engine shed at the Point.
(*Railway Magazine*/H.M.Frost coll.)

113. Surprisingly, a new 20-seater Hudswell Clarke railcar was ordered in 1933 and this and the Hardy stayed on the line until closure. During World War II, it was described as providing four miles of shake, rattle and roll, and so noisy that conversation was impossible.
(E.Codd/K.E.Hartley coll.)

114. Here is a rare view of the Hudswell Clarke railcar being driven from the 'back', ie the flat frontage end. Spurn Lighthouse and the engine shed are in the background.
(H.M.Frost coll.)

115. This is the only known photo of *Kenyon* (circa 1928) on the move with a smoking chimney. The train includes the water wagon shown in picture 112. Note the lack of any connecting rods. (E.E.Landucci/ H.M.Frost coll.)

116. This image is taken from a lantern slide. The sail wagon is on the move, probably in the mid-1920s. The Spurn sail bogies or trolleys were made out of standard platelayers trucks. See photo 117 to get a better idea of the construction and how the mast was fitted. There was something of a competition to see how many passengers and crew could travel on a single trolley. One picture I have seen shows 13 plus a dog. Not surprisingly there are several reports of people falling off en route!
(I.Massey/Scarborough Borough Council)

117. The Spurn & Kilnsea Railway was famous for the use of sail power between the wars. Here, Postman Moore is about to set off to deliver his bag of mail to the Point, the date probably being 7th October 1922. Some of the lifeboat crew are in charge of the sail. The view looks northwest into the main entrance of Godwin Fort, with the two big gun director towers visible in the background. One line curves to the left into the fort and its loading platform. The other, to the right, is the short water siding. Stopping these trolleys could be a problem and often involved pushing a railway sleeper off the front and crashing into it! (A.Clappison/H.M.Frost coll.)

118. There were at least three sail trolleys operated at various times by the lifeboatmen, the army and the lighthouse keepers. One probably started life as a pump trolley. In the past, sail trolleys were operated on railways in quite a few places in the UK and around the world. This one is seen at the Point looking west, with the estuary in the background. (C.Leonard/H.M.Frost coll.)

WORLD WAR II

119. In early 1940, Hull-based LNER Y8 class no. 559 was delivered by rail to Patrington en route for Spurn and hauled in tandem by two tractors, a modified Fordson and a three-wheeler Scammel. It was put in the charge of the Royal Engineers who nick-named it *The Black Sapper*. But with the completion of the new road in 1941, it was no longer needed and returned to Hull leaving just the Hardy and the Hudswell Clarke railcars to ferry passengers. (British Railways/K.E.Hartley coll.)

120. HRH The Princess Royal (Princess Mary) alights from the Hardy railcar on arrival within the boundaries of Spurn Fort to inspect the YMCA (Young Men's Christian Association) Centre in 1940. There was no platform within the fort. The sole Spurn Point platform was situated north of the lighthouse quite some distance away. Due to a problem on the return journey, the Hardy was pulled back by no. 559. After 1941, the railway was used less and less until closure and removal in 1951-52. (N.Redmayne/K.E.Hartley coll.)

EVOLVING THE
ULTIMATE RAIL ENCYCLOPEDIA
INTERNATIONAL

Easebourne Midhurst GU29 9AZ. Tel:01730 813169

A-978 0 906520 B- 978 1 873793 C- 978 1 901706 D-978 1 904474
E - 978 1 906008 F - 978 1 908174 G - 978 1 910356

Our RAILWAY titles are listed below. Please check availability by looking at our website www.middletonpress.co.uk, telephoning us or by requesting a Brochure which includes our LATEST RAILWAY TITLES also our TRAMWAY, TROLLEYBUS, MILITARY and COASTAL series.

email:info@middletonpress.co.uk

A
Abergavenny to Merthyr C 91 8
Abertillery & Ebbw Vale Lines D 84 5
Aberystwyth to Carmarthen E 90 1
Allhallows - Branch Line to A 62 8
Alton - Branch Lines to A 11 6
Ambergate to Buxton G 28 9
Ambergate to Mansfield G 39 5
Andover to Southampton A 82 6
Ascot - Branch Lines around A 64 2
Ashburton - Branch Line to B 95 4
Ashford - Steam to Eurostar B 67 1
Ashford to Dover A 48 2
Austrian Narrow Gauge D 04 3
Avonmouth - BL around D 42 5
Aylesbury to Rugby D 91 3

B
Baker Street to Uxbridge D 90 6
Bala to Llandudno E 87 1
Banbury to Birmingham D 27 2
Banbury to Cheltenham E 63 5
Bangor to Holyhead F 01 7
Bangor to Portmadoc E 72 7
Barking to Southend C 80 2
Barmouth to Pwllheli E 53 6
Barry - Branch Lines around D 50 0
Bartlow - Branch Lines to F 27 7
Basingstoke to Salisbury A 89 4
Bath Green Park to Bristol C 36 9
Bath to Evercreech Junction A 60 4
Beamish 40 years on rails E94 9
Bedford to Wellingborough D 31 9
Berwick to Drem F 64 2
Berwick to St. Boswells F 75 8
B'ham to Tamworth & Nuneaton F 63 5
Birkenhead to West Kirby F 61 1
Birmingham to Wolverhampton E253
Blackburn to Hellifield F 95 6
Bletchley to Cambridge D 94 4
Bletchley to Rugby E 07 9
Bodmin - Branch Lines around B 83 1
Boston to Lincoln F 80 2
Bournemouth to Evercreech Jn A 46 8
Bournemouth to Weymouth A 57 4
Bradshaw's History F18 5
Bradshaw's Rail Times 1850 F 13 0
Branch Lines series - see town names
Brecon to Neath D 43 2
Brecon to Newport D 16 6
Brecon to Newtown E 06 2
Brighton to Eastbourne A 16 1
Brighton to Worthing A 03 1
Bristol to Taunton D 03 6
Bromley South to Rochester B 23 7
Bromsgrove to Birmingham D 87 6
Bromsgrove to Gloucester D 73 9
Broxbourne to Cambridge F16 1
Brunel - A railtour D 74 6
Bude - Branch Line to B 29 9
Burnham to Evercreech Jn B 68 0
Buxton to Stockport G 32 6

C
Cambridge to Ely D 55 5
Canterbury - BLs around B 58 9
Cardiff to Dowlais (Cae Harris) E 47 5
Cardiff to Pontypridd E 95 6
Cardiff to Swansea E 42 0
Carlisle to Hawick E 85 7
Carmarthen to Fishguard E 66 6
Caterham & Tattenham Corner B251
Central & Southern Spain NG E 91 8
Chard and Yeovil - BLs a C 30 7
Charing Cross to Dartford A 75 8
Charing Cross to Orpington A 96 3
Cheddar - Branch Line to B 90 9
Cheltenham to Andover C 43 7
Cheltenham to Redditch D 81 4
Chester to Birkenhead F 21 5
Chester to Manchester F 51 2
Chester to Rhyl E 93 2
Chester to Warrington F 40 6
Chesterfield to Lincoln G 21 0
Chesterfield to Rotherham G 48 7
Chichester to Portsmouth A 14 7
Clacton and Walton - BLs to F 04 8
Clapham Jn to Beckenham Jn B 36 7
Cleobury Mortimer - BLs a E 18 5
Clevedon & Portishead - BLs to D180
Consett to South Shields E 57 4
Cornwall Narrow Gauge D 56 2
Corris and Vale of Rheidol E 65 9
Coventry to Leicester G 00 5
Craven Arms to Llandeilo E 35 2
Craven Arms to Wellington E 33 8
Crawley to Littlehampton A 34 5
Crewe to Manchester F 57 4
Crewe to Wigan G 12 8
Cromer - Branch Lines around C 26 0
Cromford and High Peak G 35 7
Croydon to East Grinstead B 48 0
Crystal Palace & Catford Loop B 87 1
Cyprus Narrow Gauge E 13 0

D
Darjeeling Revisited F 09 3
Darlington Leamside Newcastle E 28 4
Darlington to Newcastle D 98 2
Dartford to Sittingbourne B 34 3
Denbigh - Branch Lines around F 32 1
Derby to Chesterfield G 11 1
Derby to Nottingham G 45 6
Derby to Stoke-on-Trent F 93 2
Derwent Valley - BL to the D 06 7
Devon Narrow Gauge E 09 3
Didcot to Banbury D 02 9
Didcot to Swindon C 84 0
Didcot to Winchester C 13 0
Diss to Norwich G 22 7
Doncaster to Hull G 49 4
Dorset & Somerset NG D 76 0
Douglas - Laxey - Ramsey E 75 8
Douglas to Peel C 88 8
Douglas to Port Erin C 55 0
Douglas to Ramsey D 39 5
Dover to Ramsgate A 78 9
Drem to Edinburgh G 06 7
Dublin Northwards in 1950s E 31 4
Dunstable - Branch Lines to E 27 7

E
Ealing to Slough C 42 0
Eastbourne to Hastings A 27 7
East Cornwall Mineral Railways D 22 7
East Croydon to Three Bridges A 53 6
Eastern Spain Narrow Gauge E 56 7
East Grinstead - BLs to A 07 9
East Kent Light Railway A 61 1
East London - Branch Lines of C 44 4
East London Line B 80 0
East of Norwich - Branch Lines E 69 7
Effingham Junction - BLs a A 74 1
Ely to Norwich C 90 1
Enfield Town & Palace Gates D 32 6
Epsom to Horsham A 30 7
Eritrean Narrow Gauge E 38 3
Euston to Harrow & Wealdstone C 89 5
Exeter to Barnstaple B 15 2
Exeter to Newton Abbot C 49 9
Exeter to Tavistock B 69 5
Exmouth - Branch Lines to B 00 8

F
Fairford - Branch Line to A 52 9
Falmouth, Helston & St. Ives C 74 1
Fareham to Salisbury A 67 3
Faversham to Dover B 05 3
Felixstowe & Aldeburgh - BL to D 20 3
Fenchurch Street to Barking C 20 8
Festiniog - 50 yrs of enterprise C 83 3
Festiniog 1946-55 E 01 7
Festiniog in the Fifties B 68 8
Festiniog in the Sixties B 91 6
Ffestiniog in Colour 1955-82 F 25 3
Finsbury Park to Alexandra Pal C 02 8
French Metre Gauge Survivors F 88 8
Frome to Bristol B 77 0

G
Gainsborough to Sheffield G 17 3
Galashiels to Edinburgh F 52 9
Gloucester to Bristol D 35 7
Gloucester to Cardiff D 66 1
Gosport - Branch Lines around A 36 9
Greece Narrow Gauge D 72 2
Guildford to Redhill A 63 5

H
Hampshire Narrow Gauge D 36 4
Harrow to Watford D 14 2
Harwich & Hadleigh - BLs to F 02 4
Harz Revisited F 62 8
Hastings to Ashford A 37 6
Hawick to Galashiels F 36 9
Hawkhurst - Branch Line to A 66 6
Hayling - Branch Line to A 12 3
Hay-on-Wye - BL around D 92 0
Haywards Heath to Seaford A 28 4
Hemel Hempstead - BLs to D 88 3
Henley, Windsor & Marlow - BLa C77 2
Hereford to Newport D 54 8
Hertford & Hatfield - BLs a E 58 1
Hertford Loop E 71 0
Hexham to Carlisle D 75 3
Hexham to Hawick F 08 6
Hitchin to Peterborough D 07 4
Holborn Viaduct to Lewisham A 81 9
Horsham - Branch Lines to A 02 4
Hull, Hornsea and Withernsea G 27 2
Huntingdon - Branch Line to A 93 2

I
Ilford to Shenfield C 97 0
Ilfracombe - Branch Line to B 21 3
Ilkeston to Chesterfield G 26 5
Ipswich to Diss F 81 9
Ipswich to Saxmundham C 41 3
Isle of Man Railway Journey F 94 9
Isle of Wight Lines - 50 yrs C 12 3
Italy Narrow Gauge F 17 8

K
Kent Narrow Gauge C 45 1
Kettering to Nottingham F 82-6
Kidderminster to Shrewsbury E 10 9
Kingsbridge - Branch Line to C 98 7
Kings Cross to Potters Bar E 62 8
King's Lynn to Hunstanton F 58 1
Kingston & Hounslow Loops A 83 3
Kingswear - Branch Line to C 17 8

L
Lambourn - Branch Line to C 70 3
Launceston & Princetown - BLs C 19 2
Leeds to Selby and Goole G 47 0
Leek - Branch Line From G 01 2
Leicester to Burton F 85 7
Leicester to Nottingham G 15 9
Lewisham to Dartford A 92 5
Lincoln to Cleethorpes F 56 7
Lincoln to Doncaster G 03 6
Lines around Stamford F 98 7
Lines around Wimbledon B 75 6
Lines North of Stoke G 29 6
Liverpool Street to Chingford D 01 2
Liverpool Street to Ilford C 34 5
Llandeilo to Swansea E 46 8
London Bridge to Addiscombe B 20 6
London Bridge to East Croydon A 58 1
Longmoor - Branch Lines to A 41 3
Looe - Branch Line to C 22 2
Loughborough to Ilkeston G 24 1
Loughborough to Nottingham F 68 0
Lowestoft - BLs around E 40 6
Ludlow to Hereford E 14 7
Lydney - Branch Lines around E 26 0
Lyme Regis - Branch Line to A 45 1
Lynton - Branch Line to B 04 6

M
Machynlleth to Barmouth E 54 3
Maesteg and Tondu Lines F 06 2
Majorca & Corsica Narrow Gauge F 41 3
Manchester to Bacup G 46 3
Mansfield to Doncaster G 23 4
March - Branch Lines around B 09 1
Market Drayton - BLs around F 67 3
Market Harborough to Newark F 86 4
Marylebone to Rickmansworth D 49 4
Melton Constable to Yarmouth Bch E031
Midhurst - Branch Lines of E 78 9
Midhurst - Branch Lines to F 00 0
Minehead - Branch Line to A 80 2
Mitcham Junction Lines B 01 5
Monmouth - Branch Lines to E 20 8
Monmouthshire Eastern Valleys D 71 5
Moretonhampstead - BL to C 27 7
Moreton-in-Marsh to Worcester D 26 5
Morpeth to Bellingham F 87 1
Mountain Ash to Neath D 80 7

N
Newark to Doncaster F 78 9
Newbury to Westbury C 66 6
Newcastle to Alnmouth G 36 4
Newcastle to Hexham D 69 2
New Mills to Sheffield G 44 9
Newport (IOW) - Branch Lines to A 26 0
Newquay - Branch Lines to C 71 0
Newton Abbot to Plymouth C 60 4
Newtown to Aberystwyth E 41 3
Northampton to Peterborough F 92 5
North East German NG D 44 9
Northern Alpine Narrow Gauge F 37 6
Northern France Narrow Gauge C 75 8
Northern Spain Narrow Gauge E 83 3
North London Line B 94 7
North of Birmingham F 55 0
North of Grimsby - Branch Lines G 09 8
North Woolwich - BLs around C 65 9
Nottingham to Boston F 70 3
Nottingham to Kirkby Bentinck G 38 8
Nottingham to Lincoln F 43 7
Nuneaton to Loughborough G 08 1

O
Ongar - Branch Line to E 05 5
Orpington to Tonbridge B 03 9
Oswestry - Branch Lines around E 60 4
Oswestry to Whitchurch E 81 9
Oxford to Bletchley D 57 9
Oxford to Moreton-in-Marsh D 15 9

P
Paddington to Ealing C 37 6
Paddington to Princes Risborough C819
Padstow - Branch Line to B 54 1
Peebles Loop G 19 7
Pembroke and Cardigan - BLs to F 29 1
Peterborough to Kings Lynn E 32 1
Peterborough to Lincoln F 89 5
Peterborough to Newark F 72 7
Plymouth - BLs around B 98 5
Plymouth to St. Austell C 63 5
Pontypool to Mountain Ash D 65 4
Pontypridd to Merthyr F 14 7
Pontypridd to Port Talbot E 86 4
Porthmadog 1954-94 - BLa B 31 2
Portmadoc 1923-46 - BLa B 13 8
Portsmouth to Southampton A 31 4
Portugal Narrow Gauge E 67 3
Potters Bar to Cambridge D 70 8
Preston to Blackpool G 16 6
Princes Risborough - BL to D 05 0
Princes Risborough to Banbury C 85 7

R
Railways to Victory C 16 1
Reading to Basingstoke B 27 5
Reading to Didcot C 79 6
Reading to Guildford A 47 5
Redhill to Ashford A 73 4
Return to Blaenau 1970-82 C 64 2
Rhyl to Bangor F 15 4
Rhymney & New Tredegar Lines E 48 2
Rickmansworth to Aylesbury D 61 6
Romania & Bulgaria NG E 23 9
Romneyrail C 32 1
Ross-on-Wye - BLs around E 30 7
Ruabon to Barmouth E 84 0
Rugby to Birmingham E 37 6
Rugby to Loughborough F 12 3
Rugby to Stafford F 07 9
Rugeley to Stoke-on-Trent F 90 1
Ryde to Ventnor A 19 2

S
Salisbury to Westbury B 39 8
Salisbury to Yeovil B 06 0
Sardinia and Sicily Narrow Gauge F 50 5
Saxmundham to Yarmouth C 69 7
Saxony & Baltic Germany Revisited F 71 0
Saxony Narrow Gauge D 47 0
Scunthorpe to Doncaster G 34 0
Seaton & Sidmouth - BLs to A 95 6
Selsey - Branch Line to A 04 8
Sheerness - Branch Line to B 16 2
Sheffield towards Manchester G 18 0
Shenfield to Ipswich E 96 3
Shrewsbury - Branch Line to A 86 4
Shrewsbury to Chester E 70 3
Shrewsbury to Crewe F 48 2
Shrewsbury to Ludlow E 21 5
Shrewsbury to Newtown E 29 1
Sirhowy Valley Line E 12 3
Sittingbourne to Ramsgate A 90 1
Skegness & Mablethorpe - BL to F 84 0
Slough to Newbury C 56 7
South African Two-foot gauge E 51 2
Southampton to Bournemouth A 42 0
Southend & Southminster BLs E 76 5
Southern Alpine Narrow Gauge F 22 2
Southern France Narrow Gauge C 47
South London Line B 46 6
South Lynn to Norwich City F 03 1
Southwold - Branch Line to A 15 4
Spalding - Branch Lines around E 52
Spalding to Grimsby F 65 9 6
Stafford to Chester F 34 5
Stafford to Wellington F 59 8
St Albans to Bedford D 08 1
St. Austell to Penzance C 67 3
St. Boswell to Berwick F 44 4
Steaming Through Isle of Wight A 56
Stourbridge to Wolverhampton E 16
St. Pancras to Barking D 68 5
St. Pancras to Folkestone E 88 8
St. Pancras to St. Albans C 78 9
Stratford to Cheshunt F 53 6
Stratford-u-Avon to Birmingham D 7
Stratford-u-Avon to Cheltenham C 25
Sudbury - Branch Lines to F 19 2
Surrey Narrow Gauge C 87 1
Sussex Narrow Gauge C 68 0
Swaffham - Branch Lines around F 9
Swanage to 1999 - BL to A 33 8
Swanley to Ashford B 45 9
Swansea - Branch Lines around F 38
Swansea to Carmarthen E 59 8
Swindon to Bristol C 96 3
Swindon to Gloucester D 46 3
Swindon to Newport D 30 2
Swiss Narrow Gauge C 94 9

T
Talyllyn 60 E 98 7
Tamworth to Derby F 76 5
Taunton to Barnstaple B 60 2
Taunton to Exeter C 82 6
Taunton to Minehead F 39 0
Tavistock to Plymouth B 88 6
Tenterden - Branch Line to A 21 5
Three Bridges to Brighton A 35 2
Tilbury Loop C 86 4
Tiverton - BLs around C 62 8
Tivetshall to Beccles D 41 8
Tonbridge to Hastings A 44 4
Torrington - Branch Lines to B 37 4
Tourist Railways of France G 04 3
Towcester - BLs around E 39 0
Tunbridge Wells BLs A 32 1

U
Upwell - Branch Line to B 64 0
Uttoxeter to Macclesfield G 05 0
Uttoxetor to Buxton G 33 3

V
Victoria to Bromley South A 98 7
Victoria to East Croydon A 40 6
Vivarais Revisited E 08 6

W
Walsall Routes F 45 1
Wantage - Branch Line to D 25 8
Wareham to Swanage 50 yrs D 09 8
Waterloo to Windsor A 54 3
Waterloo to Woking A 38 3
Watford to Leighton Buzzard D 45 6
Wellingborough to Leicester F 73 4
Welshpool to Llanfair E 49 9
Wenford Bridge to Fowey C 09 3
Westbury to Bath B 55 8
Westbury to Taunton C 76 5
West Cornwall Mineral Rlys D 48 7
West Croydon to Epsom B 08 4
West German Narrow Gauge D 93 7
West London - BLs of C 50 5
West London Line B 84 8
West Wiltshire - BLs of D 12 8
Weymouth - BLs A 65 9
Willesden Jn to Richmond B 71 8
Wimbledon to Beckenham C 58 1
Wimbledon to Epsom B 62 6
Wimborne - BLs around A 97 0
Wirksworth - Branch Lines to G 10 4
Wisbech - BLs around C 01 7
Witham & Kelvedon - BLs a E 82 6
Woking to Alton A 59 8
Woking to Portsmouth A 25 3
Woking to Southampton A 55 0
Wolverhampton to Shrewsbury E 44
Wolverhampton to Stafford F 79 6
Worcester to Birmingham D 97 5
Worcester to Hereford D 38 8
Worthing to Chichester A 06 2
Wrexham to New Brighton F 47 5
Wroxham - BLs around F 31 4

Y
Yeovil - 50 yrs change C 38 3
Yeovil to Dorchester A 76 5
Yeovil to Exeter A 91 8
York to Scarborough F 23 9